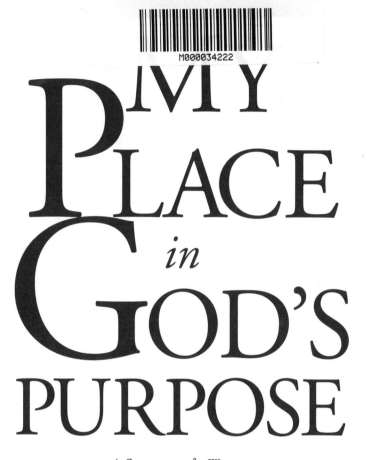

MY
PLACE
in
GOD'S
PURPOSE

A Commentary for Women
GALATIANS and EPHESIANS

Monte M. Clendinning

New Hope
Birmingham, Alabama

New Hope
P. O. Box 12065
Birmingham, Alabama 35202-2065

Cover design by Janell E. Young

Dewey Decimal Classification: 227.4
Subject Headings: BIBLE. N. T. EPHESIANS
              BIBLE. N. T. GALATIANS
              BIBLE—STUDY
              CHRISTIAN LIFE—WOMEN
              WOMEN—BIBLICAL TEACHING

ISBN: 1-56309-100-3
N944102•0694•7.5M1

Acknowledgements

I feel honored to have been asked to write this commentary for women. This would have been impossible apart from God's help and guidance from two professors at Southwestern Baptist Theological Seminary, Fort Worth, Texas: Curtis Vaughan, Distinguished Professor of New Testament and Jack W. MacGorman, Distinguished Professor of New Testament Emeritus. I am grateful for Jack MacGorman's suggestion to read through the books devotionally before research on the meaning of the Scriptures. Through this initial approach, God has given me precious insights, especially for women.

In addition, I am grateful for the influence of my home of origin; and that of my sisters in Christ in Europe, in the United States, and especially in my home church, Travis Avenue Baptist. From them and with them I continue to learn more about Jesus and how to apply His Word in my life.

Without my devoted husband's encouragement and consistent prayer support, I could never have completed this manuscript.

I express gratitude for the valuable assistance in editing from Becky Nelson and Kathryne Solomon at Woman's Missionary Union, Birmingham, Alabama.

Women of today, as you study this commentary, may God's Spirit, our promised Teacher, bring to you even deeper insights in your journey to discover and fulfill your place in God's purpose.

Monte Clendinning
Fort Worth, Texas
September 1993

Parable of the Apple Tree

The Miracle of Growth

The tree must be at least ten years old. Standing regally in the center of our backyard, its branches groan under the weight of a bumper crop of beautiful golden-red apples.

But it is not always so. Last fall and winter the branches were leafless and fruitless. We even cut away some to enhance the shape of the tree. Could there be any life left in this dark, gray-brown form?

But as spring approached, small buds appeared on the deadlike branches. Soon tiny, early-green leaves began to unfurl. Having been warmed and nourished by spring's rains and sunshine, the tree suddenly exploded in a riot of fragile, fragrant, pink and white blossoms. Had I not known fruit would follow, I might have been tempted to say, "*This* is its reason for being. What delightful floral arrangements these flowering boughs would make!" However, cutting them prematurely would have seriously marred the crop of apples to follow.

In time the blossoms faded, and the once beautiful apple tree looked like just another tree. I became impatient for fruit to appear. It's difficult to wait for maturity.

Storms came and winds blew the tree furiously, leaving a carpet of broken branches and fallen leaves at its base. But the tree stood firm. Its roots deeply penetrated the Texas soil.

One day I noticed small pea-sized green balls on the tree. Again, nourished by both rain and sun, the tiny balls slowly developed into little green apples. Week by week those small apples grew and grew, and by midsummer large ripened apples—more than ever before—covered the entire tree. Bushel after bushel was gathered by family, friends, and neighbors who ate them and made apple jelly, apple sauce, apple butter, and hot apple pies. We even froze some for future use.

Year after year the miracle of growth is repeated in our backyard. If God, from the very beginning, can place within an apple seed the complex ability to grow and bear fruit, who can doubt His ability to help us, His children, grow and bear fruit—in His likeness?

How to Become a Christian

- *God loves you* and wants you to have the best life possible (John 10:10). He wants a personal relationship with you.

- *To have the best life possible* you must have a right relationship with God. That is not possible as long as there is sin separating you from God (Rom. 3:23).

- *What is sin?* Separation from God, being interested only in your own things—not God's; anything contrary to God's standard—wrong attitudes, wrong deeds (James 4:17).

- *What is the result of sin?* Death—eternal separation from God forever in hell (Rom. 6:23; Rev. 20:11-15).

- *How can I have a personal relationship with God?* Follow His plan for salvation (John 3:16; Eph. 2:8-9).

- *What must I do?* Agree with God you are a sinner; be sorry for your sins; ask God to forgive you; believe that Jesus' death and resurrection make possible your right relationship with God (1 John 1:9; Rom. 10:9-10).

- *What then?* Ask to be baptized as a symbol of your death to an old life and your being raised to a new life in Christ (Acts 8:36-38). Join a Bible-believing church; become an active member (Heb. 10:25). Learn more about God and His plan for your life through daily Bible reading and prayer. Respond to God's power through His Spirit now within you to live with integrity and honor God. Tell others what Jesus is doing in your life (Mark 5:19; Philemon 6).

Outline of Galatians

Free to Be Me

Chapter 1—True Freedom Calls for Spiritual Growth
  I. Begins with Christ (1-5)
    A. Paul's Experience Begins with Christ (1)
    B. Paul Writes to Christians (2)
    C. Paul's Greetings Point to Christ (3-5)
  II. Avoids False Teachers (6-9)
  III. Purifies My Motives (10)
  IV. Analyzes My Religious Background (11-17)
    A. Reveals Jesus Christ (11-12)
    B. Faces Background Honestly (13-14)
    C. Talks First with God (15-17)
  V. Encourages Me to Grow (18-20)
  VI. Results in Praise to God (21-24)

Chapter 2—True Freedom Calls for Priorities
  I. Acknowledges My Significant Others (1-9)
    A. Colleagues—Barnabas and Titus (1-5)
    B. Church Leaders—James, Peter, and John (6-9)
  II. Leads Me to Service (10)
  III. Is Willing to Confront Evil (11-14)
  IV. Clarifies Salvation Through Faith (15-19)
  V. Affirms Ultimate Identification with Christ (20-21)

Chapter 3—True Freedom Does Not Depend upon Law
  I. Magnifies Faith (1-5)
    A. Question 1 (1)
    B. Question 2 (2)
    C. Question 3 (3)
    D. Question 4 (4)
    E. Question 5 (5)
  II. Reviews Our Heritage (6-14)

A. Abraham (6-9)
B. Teachings from the Scriptures (10-14)
1. Curse and the Law (10 and Deut. 27:26)
2. Righteousness and Faith (11 and Hab. 2:4)
3. Law and Life in the Old Testament (12 and Lev. 18:5)
4. Curse and Christ's Redemption (13-14 and Deut. 21:23*b*)
III. Recognizes Christ as Abraham's Descendant (15-18)
IV. Explains the Purpose of the Law (19-25)
A. To Establish a Standard Until Christ Came (19-22)
B. To Prepare Us for Christ's Coming (23-25)
V. Assures a Secure Position in Christ (26-29)
A. Races—Jew nor Greek (28)
B. Class Distinctions—Slave nor Free (28)
C. Sex Distinctions—Male nor Female (28)
D. All One in Christ Jesus (28)

Chapter 4—True Freedom Takes a Stand
I. Looks Again at Position (1-3)
II. Recognizes God's Timing (4)
A. God Has a Timetable (4)
B. God Sent His Son (4)
C. God's Son, Jesus, Was Born of a Woman (4)
D. God's Son, Jesus, Was Born Under the Law (4)
III. Discovers My True Identity (5-7)
IV. Critiques the Past (8-11)
V. May Divide Christian Friends (12-20)
VI. Respects My True Heritage (21-31)

Chapter 5—True Freedom Brings Liberation
I. Comes from My Liberator (1)
II. Brings the Only Thing That Counts (2-6)
III. Warns Against Evil Influence of Peers (7-12)
IV. Calls for Responsible Living (13-15)
V. Enables Me to Walk by the Spirit (16-26)
A. A Plea to Live by the Spirit (16-18)
B. Results of Living by the Sinful Nature (19-21)
1. Sex (19)
2. Worship (20*a*)
3. Social Relationships (20*b*-21)
C. Results of Living by the Spirit (22-26)
1. Group 1: Love; Joy; Peace (22)
2. Group 2: Patience; Kindness; Goodness (22)
3. Group 3: Faithfulness; Gentleness; Self-control (22*b*-23)

Chapter 6—True Freedom Reveals the Real Me

Book of Galatians

Free to Be Me

A Word to the Reader

Do you long to be free to be yourself—your best self? This study of Galatians is designed to help you understand what true freedom is and how you might grow spiritually toward maturity in Christ.

As you read through the book, open your heart to God. With each reading ask the Holy Spirit to teach you the meaning of that passage for your own heart. Let this be a time of study and prayer in which you move slowly through the book of Galatians, allowing God's Spirit to change anything in your life which stands in the way of your being totally committed to Him. My prayer is that your life will be so open to God that His Spirit will be able to help you through these studies to grow more like Jesus.

Each time you read the name of a city, take time to locate it on the map (p. 54) in this commentary. At the end of each chapter you will find questions for your reflection.

Introduction to the Book

Who are the Galatians? Where did they live? Some writers refer to the "northern theory"; that is, churches located in the northern part of what we now know as Turkey. A larger number of writers seem to favor the "southern theory," a group of churches in southern Galatia, then a Roman province, now Turkey. This area probably is the location of Paul's first missionary journey (Acts 13:13—14:23).

No clear date for writing this book emerges, but Jack MacGorman proposes that Galatians is pre-Romans, belonging to the period of 1 and 2 Corinthians (possibly A.D. 55-56).[1]

Why did Paul write this letter? He wrote it to defend himself and his position against his opponents. They were attacking him in two areas: (1) the authenticity of his being called an apostle; and (2) the truth of his message.

These opponents were questioning whether or not he was a real apostle. They also insisted that each Christian live under the law whereas Paul insisted each Christian should live under grace.

An understanding of key words will help unlock Paul's message for us today.

Judaizers—Paul's opponents. These were Jews who accepted Christianity, but believed that everyone should become a Jew first before becoming a Christian. They firmly believed that God's salvation was only for Jews.

Works of the Law—"Any religious system, Jewish or otherwise, whose hope for acceptance with God rests upon meritorious obedience to formal statutes."[2] Judaizers who believed Christians should live by the law meant they should become circumcised and keep all the laws of Moses. Circumcision is "a very ancient Semitic rite, involving the removal of the foreskin of male members of the community."[3] These false teachers were substituting a doctrine of salvation by works for salvation by grace.

Grace—Unmerited favor of God. Paul believed Christians lived under grace. They did not have to become Jews in order to be saved.

Perhaps the man in recent times who has best immortalized grace— amazing grace—is John Newton. Looking at the John Newton Memorial Window in the Olney, England, Parish Church, I noticed in the lower left-hand corner a slave in chains, a reminder of John Newton's former slave-trading days. On such a trip he encountered a ferocious storm at sea, which was the catalyst to draw the foul-mouthed Newton to Jesus. His life was completely changed.

In that same window one also sees the tall, erect John Newton, once slave trader now vicar of the church. From his own dark past Newton was miraculously changed by the power of God's love. Out of that transforming experience Newton penned his famous hymn, "Amazing Grace."

The word *grace* is mentioned eight times throughout Galatians. Mark this word each time you find it and notice the conditions under which it is used.

In the six chapters of Galatians, we learn that Judaizers were stirring up the Christians about how they came to be Christians. Paul contends that *all* one needs to become a Christian is to repent of one's sin and respond in faith to God through Jesus Christ.

God's Word is amazing. Even though Paul wrote this letter to the Galatians almost 2,000 years ago, its message is valid today: A person is saved only through faith in Jesus Christ.

---

[1]Clifton J. Allen, general ed., *The Broadman Bible Commentary* (Nashville: Broadman Press, 1971), vol. 11, *2 Corinthians–Philemon* ("Galatians" by John William MacGorman), 80.
[2]Ibid., 93–94.
[3]Madeleine S. Miller and J. Lane Miller, *Harper's Bible Dictionary* (New York: Harper and Brothers, Publishers, 1956), s. v. "circumcision."

1. True Freedom Calls for Spiritual Growth

I. Begins with Christ (1-5)

The very tone of Galatians in comparison with Paul's other letters leads us to realize from the beginning something is wrong. Paul seems to be defending his position as "Apostle," and he does not include his usual phrases of thanksgiving for the people to whom he writes. Clearly, he is upset.

A. Paul's Experience Begins with Christ (1)

"Paul, an apostle—sent not from men nor by man, but by Jesus Christ and God the Father, who raised him from the dead" (Gal. 1:1).

A basic definition of the word *apostle* may be found in Acts 1:21-22. Luke writes that an apostle is one who:

- was with Jesus in His earthly life
- witnessed the resurrection of Jesus

Paul did not qualify as an apostle according to this definition, for his apostleship had a greater origin than man. Greek for *apostle* means "one sent."[1] God and Jesus had called and sent him out. He had had a personal encounter with the Living Lord on the Damascus Road; no one could take that experience from him (Acts 9).

In the name Jesus Christ, Jesus is the Greek form of the Hebrew name meaning "God saves," while Christ is the Greek equivalent of the Hebrew Messiah, meaning "the Anointed One."[2]

True freedom begins with a personal encounter with Jesus Christ.

B. Paul Writes to Christians (2)

"And all the brothers with me, To the churches in Galatia" (Gal. 1:2).

Paul's inclusion of "the brothers" was probably a matter of courtesy. If we understand recipients of this letter to be in southern Galatia, the churches more than likely are Antioch (Pisidia), Lystra, Derbe, and Iconium. Notice from your map study that only Iconium (now called Konya) still stands.

C. Paul's Greetings Point to Christ (3-5)

"Grace and peace to you from God our Father and the Lord Jesus Christ, who gave

himself for our sins to rescue us from the present evil age, according to the will of our God and Father, to whom be glory for ever and ever. Amen" (Gal. 1:3-5).

Grace and peace is a favorite couplet Paul uses when writing letters. *Grace* comes from the Greek *charis,* meaning "charm or undeserved favor." Our very salvation is undeserved—that is grace. Also, grace in a Christian woman's life enables her to be more gracious. *Peace* is the Jewish word for *Shalom.* This is not the cessation of war, but a deep quietness which comes when one's heart is fully given to God the Father through Jesus Christ. Note the order: first, grace which results in peace.

Paul clearly states that Jesus gave Himself to cover our sins and to rescue us from the present evil age, or "evil eye." Who can deny that the day in which you and I live is an evil age?

How comforting it is to know that Jesus has come to rescue us from such an age. Knowing Christ personally can help us cope with our times. "Our task today is to show to our wicked world what a God-rescued and Christ-controlled life can mean in a corrupt society."[3]

Such thoughts of God's grace and peace prompt Paul to burst out in a doxology.

The woman of today who really wants to be free must have the secure foundation of a personal relationship with Jesus Christ.

II. Avoids False Teachers (6-9)

"I am astonished that you are so quickly deserting the one who called you by the grace of Christ and are turning to a different gospel—which is no gospel at all. Evidently some people are throwing you into confusion and are trying to pervert the gospel of Christ. But even if we or an angel from heaven should preach a gospel other than the one we preached to you, let him be eternally condemned! As we have already said, so now I say again: If anybody is preaching to you a gospel other than what you accepted, let him be eternally condemned!" (Gal. 1:6-9).

Paul registers his shock over how Christians could be led astray so easily by a "different" gospel. A summary of the real gospel is found in 1 Corinthians 15:3-4: (1) Christ died for our sins; (2) He was buried; (3) He was raised the third day—and all of this was just as the Scriptures had foretold. Paul was saying that this is the only gospel needed.

Paul places a dreadful curse on anyone—even an angel—who perverts the true gospel. He repeats this idea for emphasis. The woman of today who seeks true freedom will do well to look carefully at her understanding and acceptance of the real gospel, avoiding false teachers on all sides.

III. Purifies My Motives (10)

"Am I now trying to win the approval of men, or of God? Or am I trying to please men? If I were still trying to please men, I would not be a servant of Christ" (Gal. 1:10).

I was experiencing a very dry period in my Bible study when I had the opportunity to ask our visiting evangelist for his help. He suggested I rise early, ask God to lead me to a book in the Bible to read (a short one at first), and then ask Him to lead me to a verse that would be meaningful that day. I was not to read in preparation for a devotional or teaching a class. I was not to read a certain number of verses or chapters, but rather read until God's Spirit had led me to a verse which had meaning for me that day.

Following his suggestions, I selected the book of Galatians and began to read from chapter 1. My reading suddenly stopped at verse 10; in fact, that verse seemed to leap from the page. Why?

I was in my second year of teaching high school students. Throughout the year God had led me to talk privately with my students about their personal salvation. A serendipity was seeing all of them make a public profession of their faith in Christ. That summer many joined the church where I served on staff. Parents, other teachers, and people in the church began to say, "Isn't it wonderful we have this young woman here who can influence our young people in such a way!" Such words began to "tickle" my ears, and I too began to think they were lucky to have me.

As I read verse 10, God's Spirit pricked my heart, probing my motive in working with the young people. Was it for God, or was it so people would say nice things about me? His Holy Spirit helped to purify my motives that morning.

Will you allow Him to purify your motives too? Such action will move you toward real freedom.

IV. Analyzes My Religious Background (11-17)
A. Reveals Jesus Christ (11-12)
"I want you to know, brothers, that the gospel I preached is not something that man made up. I did not receive it from any man, nor was I taught it; rather, I received it by revelation from Jesus Christ" (Gal. 1:11-12).

This gospel is not something Paul, nor any other person, had made up. The biblical account of Paul's dramatic experience of grace is found in Acts 9:22-26. Paul insists he received the significance of the gospel directly from Jesus.

B. Faces Background Honestly (13-14)
"For you have heard of my previous way of life in Judaism, how intensely I persecuted the church of God and tried to destroy it. I was advancing in Judaism beyond many Jews of my own age and was extremely zealous for the traditions of my fathers" (Gal. 1:13-14).

Before conversion, Paul was a highly educated Jew, who did all he could to stamp out Christianity. Known originally as Saul, Paul was proud of his family tree. His people were Pharisees (religious leaders of the day) of the tribe of Benjamin. He was well versed in the law as well as in the knowledge of several languages.

At Jerusalem Paul studied in the rabbinical school of the Pharisees under Gamaliel, an outstanding teacher. His fanaticism caused him to aid in the stoning of Stephen, the first Christian martyr, and won him much popularity among the Pharisees. Paul thought he was doing the right thing by protecting the traditions of his family and religious teachers. At the time of his conversion on the way to Damascus, Paul was carrying letters of endorsement to bring all Christians bound to Jerusalem.

Women of today, let us examine carefully our own background. Are we Christians only because our parents are? Or have we met Christ personally? Each person must come directly to Christ—not through parents, relatives, or traditions.

C. Talks First with God (15-17)

"But when God, who set me apart from birth and called me by his grace, was pleased to reveal his Son in me so that I might preach him among the Gentiles, I did not consult any man, nor did I go up to Jerusalem to see those who were apostles before I was, but I went immediately into Arabia and later returned to Damascus" (Gal. 1:15-17).

Notice the word *but*. Often when that word is at the beginning of a sentence the remainder of the sentence is in direct contrast to the preceding words.

Paul has given us a delightful definition of conversion when he wrote, "God . . . was pleased to reveal his Son in me." Is that not what we are to be as Christians—revealing God's Son through our lives?

Notice his target group: the Gentiles. Paul, a Jew, was preaching to Gentiles—unheard of in that day! Paul had caught the spirit of the missionary message of the gospel. He came to realize God loved the *whole* world and all kinds of people who make up that world. Can we afford to do less?

After such a dramatic salvation experience, notice Paul said he did not consult any man. What do we usually do when we first have a great experience? Run and tell someone else? How human! We can learn something from Paul—first consult with God, not human beings.

No doubt Paul had to have time to sort out everything. He needed to be absolutely alone with God without distractions of any kind. Such a drastic change had come into Paul's life that he was trying to comprehend what had happened to him.

When a woman today makes a decision for Christ, she is wise to take time to think through what happened. What did God say? How did I respond? What does He now expect of me? These were valid questions for Paul and are equally important for us today. When we have an encounter with our Living God, let us, like Paul, slip away into a quiet place and allow God to help us think through what has happened.

V. Encourages Me to Grow (18-20)

"Then after three years, I went up to Jerusalem to get acquainted with Peter and stayed with him fifteen days. I saw none of the other apostles—only James, the Lord's brother. I assure you before God that what I am writing you is no lie" (Gal. 1:18-20).

After consulting with God, then Paul consulted with other people. He had a 15-day visit with Peter at which time he also saw James, the brother of Jesus. We can only speculate on what Paul and Peter discussed. Could it be Peter shared with Paul his remarkable vision and visit with Cornelius, the Gentile (see Acts 10)? Did he share the conversion of Cornelius and his household? Did he include the reaction of the circumcised believers who were with him when they saw God's Holy Spirit being "poured out even on the Gentiles" (Acts 10:45)?

Paul and Peter must have had a great deal in common as they talked of what God was doing in their lives, especially in relation to the Gentiles.

Have you experienced the sweet fellowship of sharing with a fellow believer your spiritual experience? Such fellowship can encourage you to grow spiritually.

VI. Results in Praise to God (21-24)

"Later I went to Syria and Cilicia. I was personally unknown to the churches of Judea that are in Christ. They only heard the report: 'The man who formerly persecuted us is now preaching the faith he once tried to destroy.' And they praised God because of me" (Gal. 1:21-24).

Notice Paul went to Cilicia [see-LEH-shua], the area where his hometown, Tarsus, was the capital city. It takes real courage to return to one's hometown where your former religious beliefs were well known. It takes even greater courage to face family and friends and to tell them how Jesus has changed your life—certain they will not understand.

Unbelievable! The man who once had tried to destroy Christians now is preaching the faith! Something had happened which could only be explained by the power of God at work. Recognizing God's hand on Paul, the Jewish Christians praised God for what He was doing in this apostle.

How is it with you? Do people around you praise God because of you?

11

For Your Reflection

1. What idea or Scripture verse impressed you today? Write it down.

2. Memorize the Scripture verse you wrote above. If you did not select a Scripture verse, memorize Galatians 1:10.

3. Do you have that secure foundation (salvation) as a basis for your understanding of true freedom? ___Yes ___No

   If your answer is yes, summarize your experience as follows:

   A. My life before I met Christ:

   B. What brought me to Christ:

   C. My life since I met Christ:

   If your answer is no, ask God to help you in your understanding to make Jesus Lord of your life and to repent of your sin. Read "How to Become a Christian" on page vii of this volume. Talk with your pastor or other Christian friend about your decision.

4. The word *grace* appears three times in this chapter.

   A. Write in this space the verses in which you found the word *grace*.

   B. How would you define *grace*?

5. Identify in the space below at least one area of your Christian life in which you desire to grow:

---

[1] Curtis Vaughan, *Galatians, Bible Study Commentary* (Grand Rapids: Zondervan Publishing House, 1972), 15.

[2] Madeleine S. Miller and J. Lane Miller, *Harper's Bible Dictionary* (New York: Harper and Brothers, Publishers, 1956), s. v. "Jesus Christ."

[3] *New International Version Disciple's Study Bible* (Nashville: Holman Bible Publishers, 1988), 1491.

2. True Freedom Calls for Priorities

When a woman first becomes a Christian, she is a baby in Christ. Some women, however, overlook this fact and expect to become mature instantly. Babies must have nurture and care to ensure proper growth. So it is with women who are new Christians. To reach true freedom, or maturity in Christ, one must be involved in spiritual growth. Spiritual growth calls for determining priorities in one's life.

Growth comes when one reads the Bible, prays, and exercises her faith in everyday life. Other elements also affect spiritual growth. A study of this chapter in Galatians will lead us to consider additional experiences of Paul, which could also be elements to challenge us to grow.

Notice five elements in this chapter which could lead to spiritual growth and thus true freedom: (1) significant others; (2) service; (3) confronting evil; (4) salvation through faith in Jesus; and (5) ultimate identification with Christ.

I. Acknowledges My Significant Others (1-9)

Spiritual growth does not take place in a vacuum. Often God uses other individuals to help us grow. Paul mentions several significant others in his experience:

A. Colleagues—Barnabas and Titus (1-5)

"Fourteen years later I went up again to Jerusalem, this time with Barnabas. I took Titus along also. I went in response to a revelation and set before them the gospel that I preach among the Gentiles. But I did this privately to those who seemed to be leaders, for fear that I was running or had run my race in vain. Yet not even Titus, who was with me, was compelled to be circumcised, even though he was a Greek. This matter arose because some false brothers had infiltrated our ranks to spy on the freedom we have in Christ Jesus and to make us slaves. We did not give in to them for a moment, so that the truth of the gospel might remain with you" (Gal. 2:1-5).

The first time Paul went to Jerusalem, the disciples were afraid to meet him because of his reputation of stamping out all Christians. But Barnabas believed in what God was doing in Paul's life and was willing to take Paul to the disciples (Acts 9:26-27). Barnabas had eased for Paul that first introduction to the leaders. One can readily understand why Paul chose Barnabas to accompany him on this second trip to Jerusalem.

In addition to Barnabas, Paul also took Titus, "my true son in our common faith" (Titus 1:4). Titus, unlike Barnabas, is not mentioned in the book of Acts, but Paul writes in 2 Corinthians 8:23 that Titus is his "partner and fellow worker." He seems to be a Greek convert to Christianity.[1]

Several years prior to this event Paul had listened to God when God met him and called him on the road to Damascus. Again Paul is listening to and obeying God by going to Jerusalem. Notice that Paul was not summoned by the church leaders in Jerusalem, but by God. Paul made this trip to Jerusalem to explain to the leaders privately the gospel he was preaching to the Gentiles. He seemed to be unsure as to whether or not they would accept his teachings to the Gentiles. Paul was eager to have harmony in relationships with the Jerusalem church leaders.

Verses 5 and 6 seem to be parenthetical.

False brothers, no doubt Judaizers, slipped into the ranks to spy upon the disciples. A battle, not described here, may have followed as they challenged Titus's salvation experience when he, a Gentile, had not been circumcised.

Paul was pleased that Titus was not required to be circumcised. Such action would have negated Paul's conviction that faith alone in Jesus Christ is sufficient for salvation. Paul was affirmed by the more experienced apostles.

He stood firm in his belief that a person could be saved only by faith in Christ. Gentiles need not become Jews in order to become Christians. The influential church leaders seemed to have no need nor desire to correct his teaching.

This does not mean that Paul would never preach to Jews. In fact, his pattern upon entering a city was first to go to the Jewish synagogue. This does mean, however, that his main target group would be Gentiles.

Practical lessons from this passage lead us to believe that a person does not have to do good works—or anything else—in order to earn salvation. Rather, when you accept Jesus by faith, Jesus sets you "free to attain [your] full potential."[2] Fortunate is the woman who gathers around her other significant Christians, as did Paul, who can encourage her in her spiritual pilgrimage.

B. Church Leaders—James, Peter, and John (6-9)

"As for those who seemed to be important—whatever they were makes no difference to me; God does not judge by external appearance—those men added nothing to my message. On the contrary, they saw that I had been entrusted with the task of preaching the gospel to the Gentiles, just as Peter had been to the Jews. For God, who was at work in the ministry of Peter as an apostle to the Jews, was also at work in my ministry as an apostle to the Gentiles. James,

14

Peter and John, those reputed to be pillars, gave me and Barnabas the right hand of fellowship when they recognized the grace given to me. They agreed that we should go to the Gentiles, and they to the Jews" (Gal. 2:6-9).

Paul recognized the importance of the church leaders enough for him to make a trip to Jerusalem to secure their approval of his gospel. However, his preaching the gospel of Jesus was not dependent on their approval, but God's.

The disciples came to realize God had dealt with Paul in a special way, calling him to work with the Gentiles just as they were called to work with the Jews.

Their "right hand of fellowship" simply meant an "outward token of a mutual compact or agreement."[3] This climax to the meeting showed "equality and partnership. These men pledged cooperation and mutual support in the one task of the gospel witness."[4] Paul must have felt accepted and affirmed by the staunch leaders ("pillars") of the church—James, Peter, and John.

James, Peter, and John—what an illustrious trio! James was the brother of Jesus; John was also one of the original 12 disciples; Peter, who had denied Jesus three times, later preached a magnificent sermon when thousands of people came to know Jesus. These current leaders of the church affirmed Paul in his work with the Gentiles.

Significant others in the life of a woman can also be used by God to show acceptance and affirmation of her call to serve Jesus Christ. Significant others may be such people as a parent, a mate, a sister, a brother, or a friend. When that person is a church leader, a woman is especially blessed. We place priority value on significant others who help us grow in Christ.

A significant other in my life was my mother, who herself had not come to know Christ personally until after her marriage. Not only did she teach me about Christ, but lived a life before me which helped draw me to Christ. My first understanding of unconditional love was from her. Such an experience made it far easier for me to grasp the basic meaning of God's unconditional love, although I confess I still cannot fully understand the depth of that kind of love.

As we acknowledge the place significant others have in our lives, let us also pray that we may become a significant other in the life of another Christian.

II. Leads Me to Service (10)

"All they asked was that we should continue to remember the poor, the very thing I was eager to do" (Gal. 2:10).

Paul seems to be happy about the request from the disciples to remember the poor. In fact, his future ministry indicates he actually led the Gentile churches to take an offering for the poor in Jerusalem (1 Cor. 16:1-4). Elements in one's spiritual growth are many, but one important priority to consider is *service.* Our spiritual growth should not make us an exhibit A in a spiritual growth showcase, but rather it should lead to action.

Three elements are included in a well-balanced growth process: (1) factual knowledge; (2) emotional stirring; and (3) volitional response. Women often give more attention to the first two elements without allowing an opportunity for action (volitional response). Are we deliberately making a place in our lives for service to others for Christ's sake?

Each woman needs to find her place of service in or through her church. She can, also, be assured she will have the strength to carry out what God wants her to do. William Barclay affirms this: "The man [woman] who knows he [she] has a God-given task will always find that he [she] has a God-given strength to carry it out."[5] Our lives will be a blessing to others, and we will grow through the process of serving.

Let us place priority on service. In this passage Paul mentions service especially to the poor. And in our day there is tremendous need for Christians to minister to poor people living in our areas, throughout the United States, and in foreign countries.

III. Is Willing to Confront Evil (11-14)

"When Peter came to Antioch, I opposed him to his face, because he was clearly in the wrong. Before certain men came from James, he used to eat with the Gentiles. But when they arrived, he began to draw back and separate himself from the Gentiles because he was afraid of those who belonged to the circumcision group. The other Jews joined him in his hypocrisy, so that by their hypocrisy even Barnabas was led astray.

"When I saw that they were not acting in line with the truth of the gospel, I said to Peter in front of them all, 'You are a Jew, yet you live like a Gentile and not like a Jew. How is it, then, that you force Gentiles to follow Jewish customs?'" (Gal. 2:11-14).

The Antioch mentioned here was in Syria and is the city in which disciples were first called Christians (Acts 11:26). Antioch was also the scene of this serious confrontation between Paul and Peter—the very "pillar" who had extended the right hand of fellowship earlier to Paul.

Fellowship here among Christian believers in the past had been so sweet that both Jewish and Gentile Christians began to share a fellowship meal together, a love feast—contrary to Jewish law. In fact, "a strict Jew was forbidden even to do business with a Gentile; he must not go on a journey with a Gentile; he must neither give hospitality to, nor accept hospitality from, a Gentile."[6]

The long-standing rift between Jews and Gentiles evidently had been bridged by the enthusiasm of their newfound faith in Jesus Christ.

Peter must have thought eating this love feast was acceptable, for he joined in with them until men from their top leader (James) in Jerusalem came to Antioch. These men were shocked to see Jews and Gentiles sharing a common meal. Peter became afraid for fear he would lose his good standing with Jewish Christians in Jerusalem. Therefore, he began to withdraw slowly and eat only with Jewish Christians who had also withdrawn because they were afraid of Christian Jews of the circumcision party. Obviously, Peter had a great deal of influence, for even Barnabas withdrew from eating with the Gentiles. Could it be that Peter had forgotten all about his experience with Cornelius, the Gentile, in Joppa? (Acts 10)

Paul confronted Peter. Notice his direct approach in verse 14. Jesus had died for all kinds of people. Faith in Jesus—not additional actions (such as circumcision)—brought reconciliation with God. Jesus' church should not have class distinctions in it.

The woman who desires to grow spiritually will sooner or later face the priority of confronting evil. Watch for this even among Christians. "No person no matter how respected and experienced should be followed when their direction opposes Christ's."[7]

Confronting an individual is not easy. Many women today may choose to remain silent or talk with a friend about the person causing the offense. However, confrontation often is appropriate. And the Christian woman who enters into confrontation will grow as she allows God's Spirit to guide her through such conflict.

IV. Clarifies Salvation Through Faith (15-19)

"'We who are Jews by birth and not "Gentile sinners" know that a man is not justified by observing the law, but by faith in Jesus Christ. So we, too, have put our faith in Christ Jesus that we may be justified by faith in Christ and not by observing the law, because by observing the law no one will be justified.

"'If, while we seek to be justified in Christ, it becomes evident that we ourselves are sinners, does that mean that Christ promotes sin? Absolutely not! If I rebuild what I destroyed, I prove that I am a lawbreaker. For through the law I died to the law so that I might live for God'" (Gal. 2:15-19).

Some writers call this the greatest passage in the letter. Surely we should give this top priority in our consideration of growth. In fact, if salvation through faith is not in place, there is no foundation on which one can grow. Note the meaning of key words in verse 16:

Justified—"To be declared righteous, to be treated as righteous."[8] God has said in Romans 3:23, "For all have sinned and fall short of the glory of God." Therefore, as God considers us in our natural state, we are unrighteous. But when we have faith in Jesus, we become righteous not by our strength but through the blood of Jesus Christ. Now we can stand before God "just as if I'd" never sinned.

Works of the law—(See definition, p. 6.) A shorter definition is given here: "Deeds of obedience to the Mosaic law performed with an expectation of meriting and securing a right standing with God."[9]

17

Faith—"Belief and trust in and loyalty to God."

No person is set right with God by observing the law. Righteousness can come only through faith in Jesus Christ. Law can be good and helpful, but "is powerless to save."[10]

Martin Luther, German monk and leader of the Protestant Reformation, struggled over these and similar verses in the book of Romans. Having been taught that one receives the favor of God by saying more prayers, fasting more strictly, and whipping himself more mercilessly, Luther had difficulty in understanding that salvation comes only through faith in God.

While lecturing at the University of Wittenburg on Psalms and Romans, he entitled his message "The Letter to Galatians." The words in Romans 1:17, "the just shall live by faith," and echoed in Galatians 2:16, "justified by faith in Christ," brought him the light he needed. From that time on he lived by that principle, which became one of the distinctives of the Protestant Reformation.[11]

In verse 17 Paul is incensed to think anyone would think Christ promoted sin. This is clearly foreign to the very nature of Christ. "The sin is not in abandoning the law, but in going back to the law once it has been abandoned."[12]

These verses (15-19) identify the very heart of the matter about how one becomes a Christian. Each woman, no matter how long she has been a Christian, needs to reexamine her own belief against God's standard. Is she sure her salvation comes *only* from her faith in Jesus Christ? One cannot expect to grow in the Lord until she settles this top priority.

V. Affirms Ultimate Identification with Christ (20-21)

"I have been crucified with Christ and I no longer live, but Christ lives in me. The life I live in the body, I live by faith in the Son of God, who loved me and gave himself for me. I do not set aside the grace of God, for if righteousness could be gained through the law, Christ died for nothing!" (Gal. 2:20-21).

In the past Paul had tried the way of the law; he had become highly educated in Jewish traditions; he had zealously attempted to stamp out Christianity—all to no avail.

We do not know all the experiences God used to bring Paul to his conversion, but one can believe as Paul stood and gave consent to Stephen's stoning, he was deeply disturbed by Stephen's reaction. In Acts 7:55 we learn that Stephen "full of the Holy Spirit, looked up to heaven and saw the glory of God, and Jesus standing at the right hand of God." And even during the stoning Stephen prayed, "Lord, do not hold this sin against them" (Acts 7:60).

Paul came to the time in his life when he realized that everything he could do in his own strength would never make things right with God.

The only way he could become right with God is through faith in His Son, Jesus Christ.

This intensely personal passage describes the new Paul when he denounced law and turned to Christ. The only way he knew how to relate what had happened to him was to state that his old life was dead—crucified with Christ. The old Paul no longer lives. The same zeal with which he lived his old life has been transferred to Christ as he now recognizes that Christ lives in him. In his old life, law was uppermost in Paul's life; now Christ is uppermost.

This is what always happens when a woman comes to Christ: she turns her back on her old life; she surrenders her heart and soul to Jesus; and Jesus indwells her heart and life. Paul identified with Christ both in His death and in His life. "Christ has become the source, the aim, and the motivating principle of all that he does."[13]

Paul repeats that if a person could become right with God through the law, then Christ died for nothing at all. He underscores the "superiority of the gospel of grace to the legalistic gospel of his opponents."[14]

Women of today, what do these last verses mean to us? What does it mean for us to be crucified with Christ but that we no longer live? What does it mean to us that Christ now lives in us? Are we ready to affirm this ultimate identification with Christ in our life? True freedom in spiritual growth calls for this kind of priority.

---

[1]Madeleine S. Miller and J. Lane Miller, *Harper's Bible Dictionary* (New York: Harper and Brothers, Publishers, 1956), s. v. "Titus."

[2]*New International Version Disciple's Study Bible* (Nashville: Holman Bible Publishers, 1988), 1492.

[3]Curtis Vaughan, *Galatians,* Bible Study Commentary (Grand Rapids: Zondervan Publishing House, 1972), 45.

[4]Clifton J. Allen, general ed., *The Broadman Bible Commentary* (Nashville: Broadman Press, 1971), vol. 11, *2 Corinthians–Philemon* ("Galatians" by John William MacGorman), 91.

[5]William Barclay, *The Letters to the Galatians and Ephesians,* The Daily Study Bible Series, rev. ed. (Edinburgh: Saint Andrew Press, 1983), 17.

[6]Ibid., 18.

[7]*Disciple's Bible Study,* 1492.

[8]Vaughan, *Galatians,* 52.

[9]Ibid., 53.

[10]Ibid., 54.

[11]Kenneth Scott Latourette, *A History of Christianity* (New York: Harper and Brothers, Publishers, 1953), 706.

[12]Vaughan, *Galatians,* 53-54.

[13]Ibid., 55.

[14]MacGorman, "Galatians," 95.

For Your Reflection

1. What Scripture verse or idea from this study made an impression on you? Write it down.

2. Memorize the Scripture verse you selected above. If you did not select a Scripture verse, memorize Galatians 2:20.

3. The disciples asked Paul to continue to remember the poor. Consider your service to the poor.

    A. In what way(s) am I already involved with the poor?

    B. If I am not involved, in what way(s) do I feel God could use my talents in helping the poor?

4. What would I have to give up in order to identify with Christ's death and life?

5. Write down the five priorities suggested in this chapter which challenge us to grow.

6. In which of the above areas do you feel you need to grow this year? Talk to God about this. Ask Him to lead you through experiences this year to help you grow in this area.

3. True Freedom Does Not Depend upon Law

In the introduction to the book of Galatians, we noted that Paul was defending himself in two areas: (1) his right to be an apostle and (2) the truth of his message. Chapters 1 and 2 have dealt with his response to the first of these two areas. Our attention now turns to the second area: the truth of his message.

I. Magnifies Faith (1-5)
Out of his exasperation with the Galatians, Paul asks them five questions:

A. Question 1 (1)
"You foolish Galatians! Who has bewitched you? Before your very eyes Jesus Christ was clearly portrayed as crucified" (Gal. 3:1).

Paul has discovered the Galatians are being misled to believe that to be saved they must add works of law onto their faith. He asks who has confused the Galatians or who has put the power of "an evil eye" (bewitched) on them.[1] He reminds them that Christ was clearly portrayed—put up as a poster—as crucified. Paul cannot understand why the Galatians have become confused since he had made Christ's crucifixion clear.

B. Question 2 (2)
"I would like to learn just one thing from you: Did you receive the Spirit by observing the law, or by believing what you heard?" (Gal. 3:2).

Paul calls the Galatians back to their original decision when they received the Spirit of Christ. Was it through faith or by observing the law?

C. Question 3 (3)
"Are you so foolish? After beginning with the Spirit, are you now trying to attain your goal by human effort?" (Gal. 3:3).

Paul once again shows his indignation at the Galatians for allowing this confusion to exist in their lives. He reminds them that when they began their spiritual lives (were born again) faith in Jesus was all they needed to be saved. No human effort needs to be added.

D. Question 4 (4)
"Have you suffered so much for nothing—if it really was for nothing?" (Gal. 3:4).

Paul implies that the Galatians had suffered for their original stand for Christ. Now he raises the question if their suffering was in vain.

E. Question 5 (5)

"Does God give you his Spirit and work miracles among you because you observe the law, or because you believe what you heard?" (Gal. 3:5).

A quick look into Acts 14 reminds us of the miracles to which Paul may have referred here. "Powerful deeds were not performed among the Galatians . . . because of their good works or obedience to the law. They were given by God in response to the faith of the people."[2]

Once again, women of today, we see that true freedom comes not from observance of the law, or by being involved in mere rituals, but through magnifying a simple faith in Jesus Christ.

II. Reviews Our Heritage (6-14)

A. Abraham (6-9)

"Consider Abraham: 'He believed God, and it was credited to him as right-eousness.' Understand, then, that those who believe are children of Abraham. The Scripture foresaw that God would justify the Gentiles by faith, and announced the gospel in advance to Abraham: 'All nations will be blessed through you.' So those who have faith are blessed along with Abraham, the man of faith" (Gal. 3:6-9).

To reinforce his persuasion, Paul turns the attention of the Galatians to their family tree and especially to the father of their faith, Abraham.

Reading the account of Abraham's remarkable pilgrimage of faith (Gen. 12-15) challenges us today. When God called Abraham to follow Him, He asked him to go into an unknown land. But along with that request came the promise that such obedience would be rewarded by making Abraham an instrument through which peoples of the earth would be blessed.

"God accepted Abraham's faith as equivalent to righteousness."[3] Individuals who came after Abraham could only be called children of Abraham if they had faith as he had had.

Verse 8 teaches the Galatians that God planned from the first for Gentiles to come to Him by faith. Spiritual kinship through faith in God makes an individual heir to Abraham's blessing. "All nations" indicates the missionary nature of the gospel.

B. Teachings from the Scriptures (10-14)

"All who rely on observing the law are under a curse, for it is written" (Gal. 3:10a). At this point Paul, the brilliant former rabbi, draws from his own knowledge of the Old Testament four specific teachings:

1. Curse and the Law (10 and Deut. 27:26)

"'Cursed is everyone who does not continue to do everything written in the Book of the Law" (Gal. 3:10b).

The Deuteronomy reference is "Cursed is the man who does not uphold the words of this law by carrying them out" (Deut. 27:26a).

Paul reminds the Galatians that if they revert to law only, they are living under this Old Testament curse; that is, separation from God. No person could carry out every little thing the law demanded.

2. Righteousness and Faith (11 and Hab. 2:4)

"Clearly no one is justified before God by the law, because, 'The righteous will live by faith'" (Gal. 3:11).

Almost the exact words are found in Habbakuk: "But the righteous will live by his faith" (Hab. 2:4b).

The Apostle is able to add a deeper meaning to this sentence than Habakkuk, for the Old Testament prophet had looked forward to the coming of the Messiah, while Paul had experienced Him personally through faith alone. Here *justified* seems to be equated with *righteous*.

3. Law and Life in the Old Testament (12 and Lev. 18:5)

"The law is not based on faith; on the contrary, 'The man who does these things will live by them'" (Gal. 3:12).

The Leviticus reference is: "Keep my decrees and laws, for the man who obeys them will live by them. I am the Lord" (Lev. 18:5).

This "seems to imply that even if one were able to fulfill the law, continuing in all of its ordinances perfectly, it still could not save, for the spirit of the law is antagonistic to faith."[4]

4. Curse and Christ's Redemption (13-14 and Deut. 21:23b)

"Christ redeemed us from the curse of the law by becoming a curse for us, for it is written: 'Cursed is everyone who is hung on a tree.' He redeemed us in order that the blessing given to Abraham might come to the Gentiles through Christ Jesus, so that by faith we might receive the promise of the Spirit" (Gal. 3:13-14).

The Old Testament reference in Deuteronomy is "because anyone who is hung on a tree is under God's curse" (Deut. 21:23b).

The Judaizers, Paul's opponents, had insisted that obeying the law alone entitled them to the blessings of Abraham. Paul disagrees by writing that "all who rely on observing the law are under a curse" (Gal. 3:10).

Hallelujah! We have a way out! And how is that? Christ Himself became a curse (despicable death—hung on a tree, took our curse upon Himself) that we might be redeemed (v. 13). Redeemed means "to free from captivity by payment of a ransom." Jesus became our ransom that we might be free from the captivity of sin and from living only by law (see Isa. 53:4-6). We accept this free gift by repentance and faith in Him.

Verse 14 indicates that Christ redeemed us so that Abraham's blessings could be extended to Gentiles and Jews alike. His Spirit indwells us when we have asked Jesus into our hearts by faith in Him.

God not only promised in the Old Testament that through Abraham *all* nations would be blessed, but He repeated that concept in the New

Testament: "For God so loved the world that he gave his one and only Son, that whoever believes in him shall not perish but have eternal life" (John 3:16).

Women living in modern times, we would do well to review our heritage. Are we true descendants of Abraham? You may say, "But I'm not a Jew, and Abraham was a Jew." According to Paul's teachings, if we have faith in Jesus Christ, we are a vital part of the family of faith. We receive the same blessing God promised would come through Abraham. Also, we have received the same responsibility: to be a channel of blessing to the entire world.

III. Recognizes Christ as Abraham's Descendant (15-18)

"Brothers, let me take an example from everyday life. Just as no one can set aside or add to a human covenant that has been duly established, so it is in this case. The promises were spoken to Abraham and to his seed. The Scripture does not say 'and to seeds,' meaning many people, but 'and to your seed,' meaning one person, who is Christ. What I mean is this: The law, introduced 430 years later, does not set aside the covenant previously established by God, and thus do away with the promise. For if the inheritance depends on the law, then it no longer depends on a promise; but God in his grace gave it to Abraham through a promise" (Gal. 3:15-18).

This warm term *brothers* is in stark contrast to the way Paul addressed the Galatians in verses 1 and 3 of this chapter. He follows with an example from everyday life.

When a legal document is drawn up correctly, no one can add to or take away from it. Paul explains this further by indicating God spoke His promise to Abraham. Promise "implies a giving assurance either orally or in writing but it suggests no further grounds for expectation of the fulfillment of what is promised."

Further, this promise was made to Abraham's seed, Isaac (Gen. 17:19); and through this line would come Jesus Christ, the divine Son of God, Who through His death would make it possible for all peoples of the world to be saved.

This promise was made 430 years (v. 17) before God gave Moses the law, which could not alter the earlier promise of God.

Christ is Abraham's descendant. As Christians, we are also descendants of Abraham. We do not deserve to be recipients of the blessings from Abraham. These come only through an unexpected love gift (grace) from God as we accept Jesus as our Saviour.

IV. Explains the Purpose of the Law (19-25)

Finally the question is raised in our Scriptures which we more than likely have come to ask ourselves: If we are not saved by observing the law, does

24

law have *any* purpose? If so, what?" Paul gives two answers: (1) to establish a standard until Christ came (19-22) and (2) to prepare us for Christ's coming (23-25).

A. To Establish a Standard Until Christ Came (19-22)

"What, then, was the purpose of the law? It was added because of transgressions until the Seed to whom the promise referred had come. The law was put into effect through angels by a mediator. A mediator, however, does not represent just one party; but God is one. Is the law, therefore, opposed to the promises of God? Absolutely not! For if a law had been given that could impart life, then righteousness would certainly have come by the law. But the Scripture declares that the whole world is a prisoner of sin, so that what was promised, being given through faith in Jesus Christ, might be given to those who believe" (Gal. 3:19-22).

Transgression means violation. But what was violated? In early Old Testament days, since there was no specific standard, there could be no specific violations (transgressions). But God knew His people were living contrary to the way He wanted them to live; therefore, He provided a standard (the law) by which their conduct and commitment could be judged. "Therefore the function of the law is to *define sin*. But, while the law can and does define sin, it can do nothing whatever to cure it."[5]

These laws were given to Moses long after God had made His promise to Abraham to bless all nations. The law was to be an intermediate step until Jesus came; Jesus is the only cure for sin. In Matthew 5:17 we find Jesus' relationship to law: "Do not think that I have come to abolish the Law or the Prophets; I have not come to abolish them but to fulfill them." That is, He came to fill the law full, thus becoming the permanent standard for righteousness.

Notice Galatians 3:19: A mediator put the law into effect through angels. This may refer to Deuteronomy 33:2 and Acts 7:53. Long after God had given the law to Moses, Paul may have been using the Rabbinic thought that God could not have spoken directly to man.[6] However, both Curtis Vaughan and William Barclay indicate these passages have more than 300 interpretations.

B. To Prepare Us for Christ's Coming (23-25)

"Before this faith came, we were held prisoners by the law, locked up until faith should be revealed. So the law was put in charge to lead us to Christ that we might be justified by faith. Now that faith has come, we are no longer under the supervision of the law" (Gal. 3:23-25).

Paul uses two figures of speech to illustrate this preparation for Christ's coming: Law as a (1) jailor ("held prisoners by the law") and (2) as a custodian ("put in charge to lead us"). The first, a jailor, "shows that those under the law were in a sense guarded and kept with a view to their eventually passing over into faith."[7]

The second is a custodian, who "was entrusted with the moral supervision of the child,"[8] or as Barclay clarifies, was "to take him in safety to the school and deliver him to the teacher. That—said Paul—was like the function of the law. It was there to lead a man to Christ. It could not take him into Christ's presence, but it could take him into a position where he himself might enter."[9]

But now that Christ has come we are no longer under the supervision of the custodian or the jailor—law (v. 25).

V. Assures a Secure Position in Christ (26-29)

"You are all sons of God through faith in Christ Jesus, for all of you who were baptized into Christ have clothed yourselves with Christ. There is neither Jew nor Greek, slave nor free, male nor female, for you are all one in Christ Jesus. If you belong to Christ, then you are Abraham's seed, and heirs according to the promise" (Gal. 3:26-29).

In this only reference to baptism in Galatians, Paul assures that all who have faith in and are baptized into Christ have an intimate relationship with Christ. Not only are believers intimate sons of God, but are so intimate that it is as if they are enveloped with Christ Himself.

Verse 28 is often called the Magna Carta of Humanity as it magnifies the unity all kinds of true believers have in Jesus. This does not mean that individuals lose their distinctiveness, but that in God's sight all are equal—Jew, Greek, slave, free, male, female. This verse expresses the heart of the book of Galatians: freedom for all people to reach their potential through Christ.

Christians today may have difficulty in understanding the great gulf which existed in Paul's day between races, especially Jews and Greeks (Gentiles). "The bitterest of the Jewish exclusivists maintained that God's purpose in creating the Gentiles was to provide fuel for the fires of hell."[10]

Is this a reality in today's world? Only when Christians through Christ's love and power reach out to each other do we see barriers come down.

A. Races—Jew nor Greek (28)

Barriers began to break down between races at my church, Travis Avenue Baptist, Fort Worth, Texas, on April 18, 1993. Almost 3,000 people, blacks and whites, crowded into the sanctuary to give support to "A Service of Healing and Hope for Our Community."

Sad to say, a tragedy had brought us together. Three young men known as skinheads, or white supremacists, had killed a young black man just because he was black. Two of the young men were sentenced to prison while the third received only a probation. As a result, thousands, mostly black, peacefully marched on the courthouse protesting the probation verdict.

This memorial service not only honored a young black husband who had met a premature death, but it also was an effort to show that in Christ all people are one.

B. Class Distinctions—Slave nor Free (28)

Prostitution may well be the most common form of slavery among women even today. A community minister in our city met Sara when she first came to the church asking for food and clothing. She felt accepted by the minister, whom Sara began to call the "Church Lady."

From subsequent visits, bits of Sara's unhappy story unfolded. Illiterate, more than likely on drugs, this 22-year-old who looked 45 was the only girl in a family of five. Sara received five to ten dollars a night plying her trade to earn money for food and to sustain a drug habit. She desperately wanted a baby, for she had recently lost a baby she carried when she was pushed down a flight of stairs.

Finally, she did have a baby, which Child Protective Services immediately took from her to place in custody of Sara's mother in a distant city.

This young woman joins an estimated 30 million women who since 1975 have been sold into sexual slavery.[11] Sara, made in the image of God, continues to ply this trade which enslaves her, not comprehending that God has made a provision for her to become free.

C. Sex Distinctions—Male nor Female (28)

Each sex is distinctive, but both are equal in the eyes of Jesus.

God's equality between women and men has not always been recognized. From the Jewish daily prayer book a Jewish male prays this morning prayer:

> Blessed art thou, O Lord our God, King of the universe, who has
> not made me a heathen . . . a slave . . . a woman.[12]

While traveling in various parts of the world, my husband and I have observed cultures in which women are not held in the same regard as men. This is also true in areas of our own country.

On the other hand, wherever Christ is Lord in the lives of His believers, one sees the place of women in society has been elevated. This does not mean militant feminisim, but rather godly women assuming the role God created for them.

This oneness in Christ expresses acceptance and the recognition that women, as well as men, should have the freedom to become all they can be. There is no place for competition between women and men.

My sisters in Christ, are we celebrating what Christ has done for us? He has lifted us from just being property to a place of worth. Privilege brings responsibility: to become the godly women Christ intended us to be and to share Jesus with others.

D. All One in Christ Jesus (28)

Here Paul emphasizes the unity in Christ of all races, all class distinctions, and all sex distinctions. In case he has omitted one group he uses the word *all* to cover every group. In a world in which these divisions still are seen in larger or smaller measures, this verse brings hope to each person that he or she is equal with all others in the eyes of Jesus.

In verse 29 Paul reminds us that *if* we belong to Christ—regardless of our race, regardless of our social standing, and regardless of our sex—we all are heirs of God's promise to Abraham. What freedom in Christ! Such revelation challenges us to devote our lives to sharing this message with the whole world.

For Your Reflection

1. Memorize Galatians 3:28. *There is neither Jew nor Greek, there is neither slave or free, there is neither male or female; for you are all one in Christ.*

2. List the three areas in which Paul indicates we are one in Christ. *Race, Class distinctions, Sex distinctions*

3. Write down what Galatians 3:28 means to you as a woman. *That in Jesus I am free/stand on level ground around the cross.*

Thank God for what Christ has done for you.

---

[1] Curtis Vaughan, *Galatians, Bible Study Commentary* (Grand Rapids: Zondervan Publishing House, 1972), 58.

[2] *New International Version Disciple's Study Bible* (Nashville: Holman Bible Publishers, 1988), 1493.

[3] Vaughan, *Galatians,* 62.

[4] Ibid., 64.

[5] William Barclay, *The Letters to the Galatians and Ephesians,* The Daily Study Bible Series, rev. ed. (Edinburgh: Saint Andrew Press, 1983), 29.

[6] Ibid., 29.

[7] Vaughan, *Galatians,* 71.

[8] Clifton J. Allen, general ed., *The Broadman Bible Commentary* (Nashville: Broadman Press, 1971), vol. 11, *2 Corinthians–Philemon* ("Galatians" by John William MacGorman), 103.

[9] Barclay, *The Letters to the Galatians and Ephesians,* 31.

[10] MacGorman, "Galatians," 103.

[11] Richard D. Land, "Pornography's Victims," *Salt* 3, no. 4 (1993), 2.

[12] Rev. S. Singer, trans., *The Authorized Daily Prayer Book of the United Hebrew Congregations of the British Commonwealth of Nations* (London: Eyre and Spottiswoode Limited, 1962), 6-7.

4. True Freedom Takes a Stand

Paul continues his thoughts about "heirs" from the previous chapter (Gal. 3:29). He wants to be clearly understood as the introductory words of this chapter indicate: "What I am saying is" (Gal. 4:1*a*).

Throughout this study we relate every section to our main topic, True Freedom. True freedom takes a stand as it looks again at position.

I. Looks Again at Position (1-3)

"What I am saying is that as long as the heir is a child, he is no different from a slave, although he owns the whole estate. He is subject to guardians and trustees until the time set by his father. So also, when we were children, we were in slavery under the basic principles of the world" (Gal. 4:1-3).

This passage describes a living father who wants to give his heir a settlement when the heir comes of age. Although the heir potentially will inherit the estate, as long as he is a child, he might as well be a slave so far as having access to the inheritance.

Notice the use of two words *guardians* and *trustees*. A *guardian* is "one who has the care of the person or property of another." A *trustee* is "one to whom something is entrusted." Paul indicates that the heir-child is not free to use his potential inheritance; is still under the care of a guardian and a trustee; and will be under their care until the time his father sets to give the son his inheritance.

Paul, in verse 3, refers to our being children, in slavery, and living under the ABC's (basics) of the world. This describes individuals who live under the law and not by grace.

II. Recognizes God's Timing (4)

"But when the time had fully come, God sent his Son, born of a woman, born under law" (Gal. 4:4).

These magnificent 18 words invite us to linger, to try to penetrate and absorb their deeper meaning.

A. God Has a Timetable (4)

In Old Testament times people looked forward to the fullness of time when Jesus, the Messiah would be born. In His wisdom, God knew exactly the right time to send His Son into the world. And today how comforted we are to realize that regardless of how complicated things seem in our personal world or in countries around the world, God still is in control and still has a timetable.

One of the most difficult concepts for many women to handle is waiting on God. Being a part of this "instant" generation, we want answers now—or sooner! One of the differences between false faith and real faith is one's ability to wait on God. Such faith displays maturity in one's spiritual growth.

B. God Sent His Son (4)

From the beginning of time Jesus had existed with the Father (John 1:1-2). Our minds have difficulty in comprehending that God loved us so much He sent Jesus, His only Son, into the world so that as we believe in Him, we might become rightly related to God, thereby receiving life everlasting (John 3:16). And Jesus loved us so much He voluntarily gave up His heavenly life for you and me—and all peoples of the world.

C. God's Son, Jesus, Was Born of a Woman (4)

Our minds continue to be stretched as we try to comprehend that Jesus "made himself nothing, taking the very nature of a servant, being made in human likeness" (Phil. 2:7). The Divine became also human—born of a woman. What a sacred honor! And from the time of His birth, Jesus began to elevate the place of women. Jesus—God in human form—incarnation—helps us to grasp a little more clearly Who God is (John 14:9*b*).

D. God's Son, Jesus, Was Born Under the Law (4)

Jesus was a Jew, and therefore was "subject to the restrictions, requirements, and demands of the law" just as other men.[1] Jesus can identify with all of us under bondage of the law. And why did He come? Verse 5 brings the answer.

III. Discovers My True Identity (5-7)

"To redeem those under law, that we might receive the full rights of sons. Because you are sons, God sent the Spirit of his Son into our hearts, the Spirit who calls out, 'Abba, Father.' So you are no longer a slave, but a son; and since you are a son, God has made you also an heir" (Gal. 4:5-7).

Once again Paul explains why Jesus came: to rescue all of us under law so that we might become full-fledged children (sons) of God, having an intimate relationship with Him. When we become believers in Jesus, we become sons (children) of God, and His Spirit comes to live in our hearts. God's Spirit within our hearts is evidence of our sonship.

Notice the joy a believer has in calling God the familiar term *Abba,*

Father. Abba is an Aramaic word somewhat equivalent to our English term *Daddy*. This intimate term was used by Jewish children—never servants—in addressing their father. Jesus used this same term in addressing His Father (see Mark 14:36).

Observe the progression of terms in verse 7: *slave, son, heir.* Remembering Galatians 3:28, women believers can interpret *son* as *daughter*. What an exalted privilege we have in the gospel!

When we have a tendency to become blue or depressed, let us stop to think that we women believers have discovered our true identity: We are children of the King! Let us celebrate such truth with thanksgiving!

IV. Critiques the Past (8-11)

"Formerly, when you did not know God, you were slaves to those who by nature are not gods. But now that you know God—or rather are known by God—how is it that you are turning back to those weak and miserable principles? Do you wish to be enslaved by them all over again? You are observing special days and months and seasons and years! I fear for you, that somehow I have wasted my efforts on you" (Gal. 4:8-11).

Paul describes the Galatians as slaves when they were pagans before they came to know Christ. However, when they became Christians they became released from bondage of slavery. The Apostle is asking if they now want to return to slavery under the law.

Verse 9 teaches that we are known by God. Of all religious faiths, Christianity is the only one in which God takes the initiative to reach down to an individual and offer him salvation through Jesus Christ. In all others, individuals attempt to find ways to reach out to their gods.

Paul sees the believers in Galatia as returning to a rigid observance of their special rituals: days, months, seasons, and years.

Days may have meant weekly sabbaths.

Months were probably new moons at the first of the month.

Seasons seem to have been annual feasts such as the three main feasts observed at the sanctuary by every male.

(1) Passover (Ex. 12)

Passover is the most important of the three feasts, especially for every 12-year-old male Hebrew. Its purpose was to celebrate the passing over the Hebrew houses of the death angel the night before the children of Israel were to leave Egypt for the Promised Land.

(2) Pentecost (Ex. 23:16)

In the Old Testament, Pentecost marked both a certain harvest day as well as the giving of the law at Mount Sinai.

The New Testament Pentecost, coinciding with the Old Testament day, celebrated the beginning of the church.

(3) Tabernacle (Deut. 16:13-17)

This feast, celebrated usually in the fall, corresponds to our Thanksgiving today.

Years more than likely are the sabbatic every 7 years or jubilee every 50 years.

One can almost detect tears in Paul's voice as he wonders if he has wasted effort on the Galatians.

V. May Divide Christian Friends (12-20)

"I plead with you, brothers, become like me, for I became like you. You have done me no wrong. As you know, it was because of an illness that I first preached the gospel to you. Even though my illness was a trial to you, you did not treat me with contempt or scorn. Instead, you welcomed me as if I were an angel of God, as if I were Christ Jesus himself. What has happened to all your joy? I can testify that, if you could have done so, you would have torn out your eyes and given them to me. Have I now become your enemy by telling you the truth?

"Those people are zealous to win you over, but for no good. What they want is to alienate you from us, so that you may be zealous for them. It is fine to be zealous, provided the purpose is good, and to be so always and not just when I am with you. My dear children, for whom I am again in the pains of childbirth until Christ is formed in you, how I wish I could be with you now and change my tone, because I am perplexed about you" (Gal. 4:12-20).

Paul now pleads for love and loyalty from his followers. In pleading with them to "become like me," he encourages the believers to adopt the same attitude he has toward the demands of the Jewish law: Things are different now that Jesus has come; therefore, their attitudes and actions should be different.

Writers have speculated that the illness to which he refers was a bodily ailment, eye trouble, or epilepsy. Paul may have been referring to his "thorn in [the] flesh" (2 Cor. 12:7).

The Apostle to the Gentiles simply does not understand the change in the Galatians, for earlier they would have done anything in their power for Paul. He notices (v. 15) they have lost their joy.

This is a timely word for women today. With our involvement in many endeavors, have we lost the joy we experienced on first becoming a Christian? Do other people see us as joyful believers in Christ?

Paul warns the Galatians about Judaizers who are trying to woo their loyalty away from him and the gospel of Christ. Their purpose, according to Paul, is so that the Galatian Christians might become zealous for the Judaizers.

Notice in verse 19 Paul's only use of the endearing term, "my dear children," in the entire book. In fact, he is filled with uncertainty about the whole situation and yearns to be with them. He so desperately longs for

Christ to be formed in the Galatians that he likens his own anguish over the situation to the anguish which women experience in childbirth. Paul's use of the word *childbirth* brings immediate identification for women who have borne children. We *know* the excruciating pain from such an experience. However, I wonder how many of us have agonized in a comparable way over the spiritual lostness of individuals and over those who refuse to allow Christ to be formed in their lives.

When a woman becomes serious about her commitment to Christ, such commitment may cause divisions among friends just as Paul experienced with his Galatian friends. While we always want to reach out to others in Christian love, we do not want to do so at the expense of compromising our Christian beliefs. Spiritual growth calls for us to take our stand for Christ.

VI. Respects My True Heritage (21-31)

"Tell me, you who want to be under the law, are you not aware of what the law says? For it is written that Abraham had two sons, one by the slave woman and the other by the free woman. His son by the slave woman was born in the ordinary way; but his son by the free woman was born as the result of a promise.

"These things may be taken figuratively, for the women represent two covenants. One covenant is from Mount Sinai and bears children who are to be slaves: This is Hagar. Now Hagar stands for Mount Sinai in Arabia and corresponds to the present city of Jerusalem, because she is in slavery with her children. But the Jerusalem that is above is free, and she is our mother. For it is written:

> *'Be glad, O barren woman,*
> *   who bears no children;*
> *break forth and cry aloud,*
> *   you who have no labor pains;*
> *because more are the children of the*
> *   desolate woman*
> *than of her who has a husband.'*

"Now you, brothers, like Isaac, are children of promise. At that time the son born in the ordinary way persecuted the son born by the power of the Spirit. It is the same now. But what does the Scripture say? 'Get rid of the slave woman and her son, for the slave woman's son will never share in the inheritance with the free woman's son.' Therefore, brothers, we are not children of the slave woman, but of the free woman" (Gal. 4:21-31).

Reading Genesis 16 refreshes our minds with the Old Testament account of Abraham and his wife Sarah to whom God had promised an heir. Because of her barrenness, Sarah gave her Egyptian maidservant, Hagar, to Abraham. Ishmael was born from that union. However, miraculously, God made possible a birth contrary to nature, for later Sarah in her old age became the mother of a son named Isaac.

Verse 27, a quotation from Isaiah 54:1, expands the idea of motherhood mentioned in verse 26. In Isaiah's day, the prophet describes the greatness of Jerusalem after the Exile into Babylon. The barren wife (Jerusalem) deserted by her husband after the Exile is accepted again and is "fruitful in the bearing of children."[2] Sarah, though barren at first, eventually had more children than did Hagar. "Applied spiritually, it means that the Christian community (symbolized by Sarah), though in Paul's day small and bereft of the outward glories of Judaism (symbolized by Hagar), is destined for greater fruitfulness and glory."[3]

Jack MacGorman charts the significance of these relationships as to their relevance in Law versus Grace:

Law	Grace
Hagar, a maidservant	Sarah, the wife
Ishmael, the child	Isaac, the child
Ordinary birth	Extraordinary birth
Sinai: Covenant of law	Covenant of promise: Genesis 3:15-18
Begetting slaves	Begetting freemen
Jerusalem now	Jerusalem above
They: The Jewish legalists	We: The Christian community[4]

Paul argues that those who are law-bound and reject Christ are the real descendants from Ishmael. On the other hand, the Christian community of faith receives Christ and transcends law. The Galatian converts belong to Sarah, for they are born free. Now being influenced by Judaizers these Galatian converts are threatening to remove themselves from Sarah (grace) and move under Hagar (the law).

William Barclay summarizes the meaning of this Old Testament story: "The man who makes law the principle of his life is in the position of a slave; whereas the man who makes grace the principle of his life is free, for, as a great saint put it, the Christian's maxim is 'Love God and do what you like.' It is the power of that love, and not the constraint of law, that will keep us right; for love is always more powerful than law."[5]

Women of today—true believers in Jesus Christ—are we claiming our rightful heritage and true freedom in Christ? Let us never lose sight of the fact that we are children of promise (v. 28), eternally related to the King of kings and Lord of lords. For that we take our stand!

For Your Reflection

1. What Scripture verse, or idea, impressed you most in this study? Write it down.

2. Memorize the Scripture verse you selected. If you did not select a verse, memorize Galatians 4:4-5.

3. Reread verse 19. Do you feel Christ is fully formed in you? What would your life look like if this were true?

4. What first step do you need to take to move your life toward that goal?

5. Write the name of one person for whom you are deeply burdened about Christ being formed in her or him.

6. Spend time today in praying for your own spiritual growth and that of the person mentioned in number 5 above.

---

[1]Curtis Vaughan, *Galatians, Bible Study Commentary* (Grand Rapids: Zondervan Publishing House, 1972), 76.

[2]Ibid., 90.

[3]Ibid.

[4]Clifton J. Allen, general ed., *The Broadman Bible Commentary* (Nashville: Broadman Press, 1971), vol. 11, *2 Corinthians–Philemon* ("Galatians" by John William MacGorman), 111.

[5]William Barclay, *The Letters to the Galatians and Ephesians,* The Daily Study Bible Series, rev. ed. (Edinburgh: Saint Andrew Press, 1983), 42.

5. True Freedom Brings Liberation

Chapters 1 through 4 of Galatians are devoted to doctrine, or fundamental teachings. In chapters 5 and 6 we focus on applying those doctrines. Living under grace, not under law, brings true freedom.

I. Comes from My Liberator (1)

"It is for freedom that Christ has set us free. Stand firm, then, and do not let yourselves be burdened again by a yoke of slavery" (Gal. 5:1).

Christ was liberator for the Galatians, and He is our liberator today. He has liberated us from the curse of the law of Moses—not the moral demands. The reason Christ has set us free is so that we might experience true freedom and abundant life He has promised (John 10:10b). Paul warns the Galatians, and us today, to stand firm in this freedom (grace) and let no one persuade true Christians to return to slavery (law).

We are living in an age where in some places the role of women seems to be uncertain. This passage indicates to me that when we once become liberated by Christ, we recognize our worth to Him and to His world. Our self-esteem rises and, regardless of the area in which we find ourselves (home, office, school, etc.), we can now hold our heads up with the assurance each of us is special and has a unique contribution to make to God's world. Such an experience does not allow for militant aggressiveness, but rather a gracious confidence originating in the heart of our liberator, Jesus Christ.

II. Brings the Only Thing That Counts (2-6)

"Mark my words! I, Paul, tell you that if you let yourselves be circumcised, Christ will be of no value to you at all. Again I declare to every man who lets himself be circumcised that he is obligated to obey the whole law. You who are trying to be justified by law have been alienated from Christ; you have fallen away from grace. But by faith we eagerly await through the Spirit the righteousness for which we hope. For in Christ Jesus neither circumcision nor uncircumcision has any value. The only thing that counts is faith expressing itself through love" (Gal. 5:2-6).

Paul pointedly speaks to the Galatians against allowing themselves to be circumcised to ensure becoming a *real* Christian, which would put them into a position to have to obey the whole law. Circumcision under such conditions has no value as far as becoming a Christian is concerned. The hope of righteousness (v. 5), Paul writes, comes only through faith in Jesus Christ.

An interesting triad seen here, which also appears throughout Paul's writings, is faith, hope (v. 5), and love (v. 6). Perhaps the best-known triad is found in 1 Corinthians 13:13: "And now these three remain: faith, hope and love. But the greatest of these is love."

While the Apostle shares with the Corinthians his belief that the greatest of the triad is love, in this letter to the Galatians (5:6) he states another dimension: Faith expressing itself through love is the *only* thing that counts. "Faith is glad and trusting response to God's outreaching grace in Jesus Christ."[1] And this faith works through the medium of love.

Women of today, think of the tremendous impact our lives could have in our world if we lived out our faith through love. This type of love is agape—God's unselfish, unconditional love. Our world desperately needs to experience this revolutionary kind of love. Paul tells us that is the only thing that counts. Is this a priority in our lives?

Such a priority was Lou Heath's life when she took a hot dish to Ammurate [ahm-u-RAH-te], an Indian woman suffering complications following the birth of her first child. Ammurate was a member of Lou's internationals mission action group at her church. "O God," Lou prayed before entering the small apartment, "help me to show them You really love them."

This prayer resulted in Lou's keeping the newborn baby for months; an entire Baptist church's becoming involved in ministering to the stricken family; Lou's having an opportunity to share Christ with the new mother on her deathbed; and the largest group ever of Indian students living in Tennessee to gather for the mother's memorial service in a Baptist church where they also heard a clear presentation of the gospel. And it all began when one woman took seriously the command of Jesus to love the people of the world.

III. Warns Against Evil Influence of Peers (7-12)

"You were running a good race. Who cut in on you and kept you from obeying the truth? That kind of persuasion does not come from the one who calls you. 'A little yeast works through the whole batch of dough.' I am confident in the Lord that you will take no other view. The one who is throwing you into confusion will pay the penalty, whoever he may be. Brothers, if I am still preaching circumcision, why am I still being persecuted? In that case the offense of the cross has been abolished. As for those agitators, I wish they would go the whole way and emasculate themselves!" (Gal. 5:7-12).

Paul commends the Galatians until someone (Judaizers) interfered with their Christian walk by insisting they should be circumcised.

Notice Paul's proverb in verse 9, quoted also in 1 Corinthians 5:6. *Yeast in the Bible is usually a symbol for evil, and here refers to Judaizers.* (Matt. 13:33 and its parallel in Luke 13:21 are exceptions.) Have you made yeast bread recently? Surely you have noticed how the yeast permeates all other ingredients. In the same manner the message of the evil Judaizers will permeate the Christian community unless their actions are stopped.

In verse 10 we see Paul's confidence is from the Lord. He asserts that those who throw these Christians into confusion will receive their own penalty.

Verse 11 seems to imply that circumcision to the Judaizers has the same place that the Cross of Christ has to Paul. Circumcision and the Cross are contradictory to each other.

Take care in verse 12 to realize Paul does not really mean he wants the Judaizers to mutilate themselves, but he "uses mocking satire to point up the logical issue of the Judaizers' veneration for circumcision."[2] He may have been alluding to the self-mutilation engaged in by the priests of Cybele, goddess in Greek mythology, who had one of her most important worship centers in Galatia.

This passage warns us against well-meaning peers who try to pull us away from our basic faith.

IV. Calls for Responsible Living (13-15)

"You, my brothers, were called to be free. But do not use your freedom to indulge the sinful nature; rather, serve one another in love. The entire law is summed up in a single command: 'Love your neighbor as yourself.' If you keep on biting and devouring each other, watch out or you will be destroyed by each other" (Gal. 5:13-15).

For many of us the word *freedom* does not have the depth of meaning as it does to people living in another culture. In 1960 I stood in a circle of Baptist women in Switzerland who had gathered from various parts of Europe. Holding hands, we sang—each in her own language—"Blest Be the Tie." I was deeply moved especially when I saw tears streaming down the faces of women from Eastern Europe. More than likely they realized this could be the only time they would be allowed to leave their country to have fellowship with Christian sisters. Oh, how sweet true freedom can be!

However, freedom does not mean one is free to do whatever one desires. Freedom also brings responsibility. In verse 13 Paul cautions Galatian Christians not to engage in sinful practices, but to look for ways to serve one another in love.

The Apostle has spent much effort in this letter trying to teach the Galatians limitations of the law. Notice how he pointedly asserts that "the entire law is summed up in a single command" (v. 14). Modern-day

Christians recognize that command, "Love your neighbor as yourself," as coming from Jesus, Who quoted from the heart of the Mosaic law, Leviticus 19:18. In his gospel Luke records Jesus' encounter with an expert in the law who asked, "Who is my neighbor?" Jesus answered by telling the parable of the good Samaritan (Luke 10:25-37).

Freedom is thwarted when Christians bite and devour each other like wild animals in a death-like struggle. How can one avoid this? Watch for answers in the remainder of this chapter.

V. Enables Me to Walk by the Spirit (16-26)
A. A Plea to Live by the Spirit (16-18)
"So I say, live by the Spirit, and you will not gratify the desires of the sinful nature. For the sinful nature desires what is contrary to the Spirit, and the Spirit what is contrary to the sinful nature. They are in conflict with each other, so that you do not do what you want. But if you are led by the Spirit, you are not under law" (Gal. 5:16-18).

Verse 16 contains both a command and a promise: Command—"live by the Spirit"; promise—"and you will not gratify the desires of the sinful nature."

How can one avoid living the sinful life? "Live by the Spirit" is the antidote. This word *live* means "to keep on living." This is continuous action—not a onetime process. When one allows her sinful nature to be in control, only conflict can result, for God's Spirit and sinful nature are directly opposite. How can one avoid this miserable situation? Allow God's Spirit, Who is already within the life of a Christian, to be in control at all times. Such action ensures the individual is not under law.

B. Results of Living by the Sinful Nature (19-21)
"The acts of the sinful nature are obvious: sexual immorality, impurity and debauchery; idolatry and witchcraft; hatred, discord, jealousy, fits of rage, selfish ambition, dissensions, factions, and envy; drunkenness, orgies, and the like. I warn you, as I did before, that those who live like this will not inherit the kingdom of God" (Gal. 5:19-21).

This listing is not exhaustive (v. 21), but rather includes some of the more common results of sinful living in Paul's day. Is this relevant for women today?

Women of today, look around us. On every hand we see modern-day women involved in many of the same things Paul described in these verses. Paul's list, written almost 2,000 years ago, is as up-to-date as today's tabloids. When will we take Christ's standards for our lives seriously?

Jack MacGorman separates this list into three categories: sex; worship; and social relationships.[3]

1. Sex (19)
• Sexual immorality is sexual conduct in discord "with accepted ethical

principles or the dictates of conscience." Sex in itself is not evil. In fact, God made sex for man and woman to experience the deepest human relationship within the bonds of marriage.

Individuals who engage in sex outside of marriage (premarital or extramarital) miss God's purpose of deepest satisfaction within the sanctity of a permanent relationship between one man and one woman. "The one completely new virtue Christianity brought into the world was chastity."[4]

• Impurity—William Barclay describes impurity as "that which makes a man unfit to come before God, the soiling of life with the things which separate us from him."[5] The times in which we live reflect a frightening attitude toward the sacredness of sex. Countless individuals seem to disregard the danger of sexually transmitted diseases.

• Debauchery is "extreme indulgence in sensuality." This is sexual relations gone wild, perverted, without any sense of decency.

The sin of homosexuality "had swept like a cancer through Greek life and from Greece, invaded Rome. . . . In the time of the Early Church, the world was lost to shame; and there can be little doubt that this was one of the main causes of its degeneracy and the final collapse of its civilization."[6] Will this be the fate of our country? Today's world is attempting to redefine the meaning of adultery, prostitution, and homosexuality. But God's Word has not changed; they all are still sin.

2. Worship (20a)

The second category of living according to sinful nature relates to worship stated in two ways: idolatry and witchcraft.

• Idolatry is "the worship of a physical object as a god." Watch this one! Idolatry can be very subtle. We may say we do not worship an idol fashioned by men's hands, but what about the physical object to which we give large portions of our time and/or our money? That is an idol.

• Witchcraft is "sorcery or any kind of magic art."[7] Sorcery is "the use of power gained from the assistance or control of evil spirits." Originally the word *witchcraft* came from the same Greek word from which comes the word *pharmacy*, which is related to drugs, or the use of drugs.[8]

Paul says that witchcraft is sinful and is to be avoided. This includes such practices as Satan worship, the occult, drug abuse, dependence on horoscopes, or anything that attempts to move our minds beyond their normal capability. A 1993 daily newspaper carried an article in which a coven of witches desired to open a private school. In addition to a regular school curriculum, a priestess said, "It gives us the chance for our children to not be exposed to things that we feel are detrimental, like the Christian values or the Hollywood version of the bad witch."[9]

3. Social Relationships (20b-21)

Women (and men) are created to be social beings, not living in isolation. However, when our lives are controlled only by our sinful nature, Paul warns that these nine sins can occur:

- Hatred is "prejudiced hostility." This shows itself in a person who basically is hostile to people.
- Discord means "a lack of agreement or harmony (as between persons, things, or ideas)."
- Jealousy is hostility "toward a rival or one believed to enjoy an advantage."
- Fits of rage are acts of impulsive and irregular "violent and uncontrolled anger."
- Selfish ambition is "an ardent desire for rank, fame, or power" (personally).
- Dissensions are akin to "discord," but can include "contentious quarreling."
- Factions are parties or groups which are often "contentious or self-seeking." Women should be able to respect women with different views from their own; when this does not happen, factions can occur.
- Envy means "painful or resentful awareness of an advantage enjoyed by another joined with a desire to possess the same advantage." This describes the individual who even grieves when another person has an advantage.
- Drunkenness and orgies mean out-of-control drinking and carousing.

Notice the stern warning the Apostle gives in the latter part of verse 21 that individuals who engage in these practices "will not inherit the kingdom of God." Paul refers to the individual who makes a habit of these things, showing no evidence of a genuine conversion experience. Such a condition is different from an occasional slip which Vaughan recognizes could happen to a Christian who gives in to temptation.[10]

C. Results of Living by the Spirit (22-26)

"But the fruit of the Spirit is love, joy, peace, patience, kindness, goodness, faithfulness, gentleness and self-control. Against such things there is no law. Those who belong to Christ Jesus have crucified the sinful nature with its passions and desires. Since we live by the Spirit, let us keep in step with the Spirit. Let us not become conceited, provoking and envying each other" (Gal. 5:22-26).

How grateful we are Paul did not end the fifth chapter of Galatians with verse 21! Life does not have to be lived on that sinful plane. Jesus Christ offers more—so much more! And when life is lived in the Spirit, one's life shows "the outworking of an indwelling Presence, not the imposing of a higher legalism."[11]

Paul describes nine qualities of life which can be expected to result from living by the Spirit. He calls them "fruit" listed below in three groups:

1. Group 1: Love; Joy; Peace (22)

- Love—The Greek word here is *agape*. William Barclay translates this type of love as "unconquerable benevolence."[12] The idea is that person 1 wants the very best for person 2, regardless of what it costs person 1.
- Joy—The Greek word here is *chara*. Most authorities agree that this type of joy is based on a personal relationship with God through Jesus.

MacGorman comments, "So deep is its wellspring located in God's grace that even the most adverse circumstances cannot stanch its flow."[13]

- Peace—*Eirene* is Greek for peace while *shalom* is the Hebrew counterpart. The meaning in this context seems to be not just the absence of conflict, but the presence of everything that would make for the highest good of an individual. Thus a serenity is in a Christian's heart as she realizes that her times are in God's hands (see Psalm 31:15*a*).

2. Group 2: Patience; Kindness; Goodness (22)

- Patience—Patience means having a long fuse. Just as God is able to wait, to give us a second chance, so can a Christian through God's Spirit have the ability to wait.
- Kindness—Kindness is a characteristic which reflects an interest in another person's well-being. A kind person is not a weak person, but is a thoughtful individual.
- Goodness—This word suggests generosity and appears only four times in the New Testament—all in Paul's writings.

3. Group 3: Faithfulness; Gentleness; and Self-control (22*b*-23)

- Faithfulness—*Fidelity* is another word for *faithfulness*. It suggests reliability.
- Gentleness—Being considerate is one characteristic of this fruit of the Spirit. Gentleness is not a sign of weakness, but rather tenderness shown at the appropriate time. Jesus, our example, was gentle with the woman caught in adultery; but He displayed His wrath when the Temple was defiled.
- Self-control—Barclay writes, "It is the virtue which makes a man so master of himself that he is fit to be the servant of others."[14]

What a beautiful contrast Paul gives of verses 22-23 as over against verses 19-21! He emphasizes that there is no law against such things as the fruit of the Spirit.

How can women grow spiritually so as to produce the fruit of the Spirit? The answer is found in verse 24: Belong to Christ and therefore each person, through the power of God's Spirit, will be able to crucify her sinful nature. Such fruits as described above do not automatically happen. We must deliberately decide to allow Christ to take charge of our lives so that they might glorify Him in all we do. Thus, we can avoid being conceited, and provoking each other.

Paul concludes chapter 5 by encouraging all of us not only to live by the Spirit, but also to keep step with the Spirit. To keep step with the Spirit means to make progress as on a journey.

Women of today, we *can* grow spiritually. Before we grow, we must be sure we are born spiritually (repent of our sins, trust Jesus to save us, and accept His gift of eternal life). Then we must concentrate on growing as Christians.

Such growth calls for diligent Bible study to learn what God is expecting of us; praying regularly to our heavenly Father; putting Him first in our lives; and living each day in such a way that would please God. Spiritual growth calls for confession of sin daily and accepting God's forgiveness (1 John 1:9). God causes growth to occur.

As we allow His Spirit to direct us, more fruit will be seen in our lives. Walking by the Spirit should not be for the exceptional Christian, but for the normal Christian life.

Let us be so filled with God's Spirit that much fruit will be seen in our lives. How beautiful is a spirit-filled woman! Such a woman will experience true freedom.

[1]Clifton J. Allen, general ed., *The Broadman Bible Commentary* (Nashville: Broadman Press, 1971), vol. 11, *2 Corinthians–Philemon* ("Galatians" by John William MacGorman), 115.

[2]Curtis Vaughan, *Galatians, Bible Study Commentary* (Grand Rapids: Zondervan Publishing House, 1972), 98

[3]MacGorman, "Galatians," 118-19.

[4]William Barclay, *The Letters to the Galatians and Ephesians*, The Daily Study Bible Series, rev. ed. (Edinburgh: Saint Andrew Press, 1983), 46.

[5]Ibid., 47.

[6]William Barclay, *The Letters to the Corinthians*, The Daily Study Bible Series, rev. ed. (Edinburgh: Saint Andrew Press, 1984), 53-54.

[7]Vaughan, *Galatians*, 104.

[8]Ibid.

[9]Erin Hallissy, "Witches Want School If California Voucher Plan Passes," *Fort Worth Star-Telegram*, Saturday, July 17, 1993, sec. A, 15.

[10]Curtis Vaughan, conversation with writer, June 7, 1993.

[11]MacGorman, "Galatians," 119.

[12]Barclay, *Galatians*, 50.

[13]MacGorman, "Galatians," 119.

[14]Barclay, *Galatians*, 52.

For Your Reflection

1. Write down the idea or Scripture verse which most impressed you from this study.

2. Memorize the Scripture verse mentioned in number 1 above. If you did not select a verse, memorize Galatians 5:6*b*.

3. Reread verses 19-21. Write the list of sins in this space.

   Place a check mark by the sin(s) from this list in your own life. Confess them now and move through the process described in 1 John 1:9.

4. Reread verses 22-23. Write the list of fruit of the Spirit in this space.

   Place a plus mark (+) by the fruit you are aware of in your life now. Thank God for His blessings.

   Place a check mark by the fruit in which you want to grow more. Talk to God about your desires. Ask Him to direct you.

6. True Freedom Reveals the Real Me

In chapter 5 Paul has just challenged Galatian Christians to walk in the Spirit, thus producing in their lives fruit of the Spirit. In chapter 6 he gives them practical guidance in living out the Spirit-filled life.

I. Finds Expression in a Love-filled Life (1-10)
A. When Someone Sins (1)

"Brothers, if someone is caught in a sin, you who are spiritual should restore him gently. But watch yourself, or you also may be tempted" (Gal. 6:1).

Paul has softened his tone again in calling the Galatians brothers. Living a Spirit-filled life does not mean living an isolated life. Rather we are to interact with others and become "salt of the earth" (Matt. 5:13). One of the qualities of salt is curative, a characteristic of restoration mentioned in verse 1.

Notice that we are to be gentle—not judgmental—as we attempt, through God's help, to restore a person who has slipped. We are to be constructive, endeavoring to help an individual as carefully as sailors mend their nets or doctors set a broken bone.

But there is a word of caution: Watch yourself. Just because God is allowing us to help the person who sins does not ensure we ourselves will not be tempted. Satan is ever ready to lure us into sin.

A young married seminarian attempted to counsel a young divorcée about her family problems. His intent was good, but in the process he became infatuated with the woman and plunged himself and his own family into devastating problems. Paul gives a warning against this kind of action.

B. In Carrying Burdens of Others (2)

"Carry each other's burdens, and in this way you will fulfill the law of Christ" (Gal. 6:2).

One of the joys of being a Christian is to help other people when they are in need. Especially is this true when members of a Sunday School class or another unit in a church help carry the heavy burden of a fellow member. In doing this we are fulfilling the law of Christ (love) rather than the legalistic system of the Judaizers.

C. In Avoiding Conceit (3-4)

"If anyone thinks he is something when he is nothing, he deceives himself. Each one should test his own actions. Then he can take pride in himself, without comparing himself to somebody else" (Gal. 6:3-4).

Webster defines *conceit* as "excessive appreciation of one's own worth or virtue." Proverbs 16:18 indicates the result of such conceit: "Pride goes before destruction, a haughty spirit before a fall."

A fine line exists between a healthy self-image and pride. Having been made in the image of God and having been redeemed by Jesus, Christian women today have every right to have a healthy self-image.

Pride, on the other hand, is smugness when one cannot imagine having faults and weaknesses as some others. As this Scripture verse indicates, this kind of person deceives herself.

How do we handle such a condition? God tells us to examine ourselves vigorously. We need to test ourselves against the highest we can achieve—not by belittling others.

D. In Carrying One's Own Burden (5)

"For each one should carry his own load" (Gal. 6:5).

The latter part of verse 5 may seem a contradiction to the thought in verse 2 relative to burden bearing. While two different Greek words are used, there is very little difference in their meaning.[1] The distinction comes first (v. 2) in burdens which *can be* shared; and second (v. 5), burdens which an individual *should* bear himself.

E. In Relating to Our Teachers (6)

"Anyone who receives instruction in the word must share all good things with his instructor" (Gal. 6:6).

In early Christian days pagans were not taught by priests nor did they pay them. However, when Christian teachers began to emerge, Paul instructed Christians to share not only material things, but "all good things." This verse is a basis today for paying our Christian teachers and leaders.

F. In Our Actions (7-8)

"Do not be deceived: God cannot be mocked. A man reaps what he sows. The one who sows to please his sinful nature, from that nature will reap destruction; the one who sows to please the Spirit will reap eternal life" (Gal. 6:7-8).

Paul gives a warning here that God cannot be mocked or be treated with contempt. He illustrates this concept with the Law of the Harvest: What you sow you also reap.

What a strange thing it would be if when we planted seeds labeled Flowers, vegetables grew instead! When we plant flower seeds, we expect flowers to grow.

So it is in our spiritual lives. When we sow sin as described in Galatians 5:19-21, that kind of sin is seen in our lives.

On the other hand, when we sow things of the Spirit, spiritual fruit will result (see Gal. 5:22-23). Notice that things of the spirit result in eternal life. This is not just everlasting life after we die, but eternal life begins the instant we receive Jesus by faith into our lives. Our quality of life becomes richer and more productive on this earth.

G. In Being Persistent (9)

"Let us not become weary in doing good, for at the proper time we will reap a harvest if we do not give up" (Gal. 6:9).

Many of us, no doubt, identify with doing our best on a special project for the Lord, and yet results do not seem to match the amount of energy expended.

God's Word encourages us not to become weary. A promise follows: In the proper time we *will* reap a harvest if we continue to be faithful.

Missionaries today in certain parts of the world can identify with and receive encouragement from this idea. For example, those who serve diligently in Japan where results are very slow could become quite discouraged when they learn of the large numbers of new believers baptized in 1993 in Kenya.

The need for persistence is seen not only on the missions field but also in the Christian woman who desires to make a difference in her home or her workplace. Many woman today are wearing multi-hats; stress levels can run high from daily demands of family and work. God's promise is to all who continue to do their best and continue to persist. The harvest will come in the proper time. Our task is to be faithful.

H. In Doing Good to All (10)

"Therefore, as we have opportunity, let us do good to all people, especially to those who belong to the family of believers" (Gal. 6:10).

Paul continues to encourage the Galatian Christians, and us today, to live out the life of love. Very practically, he suggests that we become sensitive to opportunities to help people of all kinds. Jesus is our example as we reflect on how He helped all kinds of people such as Pharisees, Samaritans, blind, lame, and sinners.

While we are instructed to watch for opportunities to do good to all people, to encourage and minister in times of crisis, we are also told not to overlook those in our own family of faith. This includes family members and our church members as well as the larger family of believers beyond our own church. In fact, we are to take positive action to strengthen all such relationships.

These eight practical illustrations give us clues as to how we can live out the life of love as we walk in the Spirit. Let us give close attention to these specific guidelines as we seek to grow spiritually, becoming more like Jesus.

II. May Bring Controversy (11-13)

"See what large letters I use as I write to you with my own hand! Those who want to make a good impression outwardly are trying to compel you to be circumcised. The only reason they do this is to avoid being persecuted for the Cross of Christ. Not even those who are circumcised obey the law, yet they want you to be circumcised that they may boast about your flesh" (Gal. 6:11-13).

Verse 11 begins the closing portion of Paul's letter to the Galatians. Many writers think Paul's eyesight was beginning to dim; therefore, he is writing in very large letters. Usually he took the pen from his secretary and signed his own name, but for some reason in this letter he did more.

He returns to his original theme and concern: Judaizers were insisting Galatian Christians also had to be circumcised to be real Christians. Paul contends that faith in Jesus is all one needs.

Official Judaism would recognize a Christian belief which included circumcision of the Gentile converts. MacGorman writes, "This would have removed 'the stumbling block of the cross'"(5:11*b*).[2] Paul accuses the Judaizers of boasting about circumcised Gentiles, but not keeping their own law. When women become Christians, such action may cause controversy in the community in which they live, especially if people there are not clear on how to become a Christian.

III. Refines My Boasting (14)

"May I never boast except in the cross of our Lord Jesus Christ, through which the world has been crucified to me, and I to the world" (Gal. 6:14).

Paul refers to boasting in a positive way: He boasts about the Cross of Christ—not about what he himself has done. We, along with Paul, have every right to boast about the Cross of Jesus—not the wooden crucifix itself, but the love shown as Jesus paid our sin debt when He died on the Cross.

One April afternoon I boasted in the Cross as I lifted my eyes to a cross on top St. Paul's facade towering over the marketplace in Macao, a small Portuguese colony on mainland China. I was told that cross on top of the ruins of St. Paul's Cathedral had earlier provided inspiration to a former mayor of Hong Kong to write the hymn "In the Cross of Christ I Glory."[3]

I saw some of the changes the Christ of the Cross had brought to that small colony as missionaries faithfully witnessed to thousands of Chinese, many of whom had become believers. In spite of living on a meager income, these Chinese believers have experienced an unbelievable freedom in Christ. Yes, I boasted in the Cross!

IV. Makes Me a New Creation (15-16)

"Neither circumcision nor uncircumcision means anything; what counts is a new creation. Peace and mercy to all who follow this rule, even to the Israel of

50

God" (Gal. 6:15-16).

What really counts in our spiritual lives is not ritual or legalism, but the fact that when we become believers in Christ we become new creations.

Yesterday, as a young seminary student helped me plant shrubs in our yard, he said, "God is good. It's a miracle I'm in the seminary at all. God has changed my life. If you really knew about my wicked past, you probably would not even want me in your yard." Together we rejoiced that God had made each of us a new creation.

V. Carries Marks of the Christian (17-18)

Paul brings to a close this letter to the Galatians by writing, *"Finally, let no one cause me trouble, for I bear on my body the marks of Jesus. The grace of our Lord Jesus Christ be with your spirit, brothers. Amen" (Gal. 6:17-18).*

More than likely one could see on Paul's body the scars left from beatings and stonings he had received because he was a devout follower of Jesus Christ.

You and I may never bear such scars on our outward body from persecution. However, many Christian women do bear scars within, such as wounded spirits from discrimination, lack of understanding, and emotional support from family members and supervisors who simply do not understand what Christian commitment means.

There is one distinctive mark which should be worn proudly by every believer in Jesus Christ, male or female; and that is agape, the Christlike love—unselfish, sacrificial, always wanting the very best for the other person.

This kind of love is accepting and forgiving. It builds up others—never tears them down, especially behind their backs. And agape always takes the initiative to right some wrong.

Women of today, is this the kind of mark we bear as we live out our faith in our family, in the neighborhood, at the workplace, and in relating to strangers? Such love shows real maturity in Christ. This can be ours when we allow Jesus to take first place in our lives.

One can detect warmth and love in his voice as Paul pens his closing sentence of this letter. For the eighth time the word *grace* appears. Paul yearns for his fellow believers to experience the "grace of our Lord Jesus Christ"—by faith alone, simply, profoundly, unhampered by rituals or legalism. He knew, as we know today, the transforming power of God's grace.

This marvelous grace I have seen in the life of a sister in Christ. Barbara and I have worked together and prayed together in women's work in our church. As a leader, she is attractive, creative, gracious, always well-dressed, and her lovely home looks as if it might be featured in *House Beautiful.*

Her husband is also active in the church. One son is a minister, and all the children are involved in church. They are a close-knit, loving family. Surely Barbara must have been born with a silver spoon in her mouth!

As she shared with me some of her background, I was utterly astonished. Born into the home of an alcoholic father and a mother with fragile health, Barbara is the oldest of three children. Living in a government housing area as a little girl, she played at the area recreation center, which on Sunday held Sunday School led by a retired missionary and his wife. This young girl began to attend, and one Sunday she responded to the missionary's invitation to ask Jesus into her heart.

Later she dropped out of high school and traveled to a distant state to visit her grandparents, who kept her, loved her, and nurtured her. Barbara met her future husband, also a Christian, in church. Soon they were married and established their own Christian home. With encouragement from her husband, she finished college and then received her master's degree.

Barbara's deep desire is that other women too may come to know Jesus personally and also experience His amazing grace.

God's grace does not assure an individual wealth and ease, but it does assure that God seeks only His highest good for that one who trusts in Him.

None of us deserves God's grace, but He gives it freely to those who open their hearts to Him. He continues to pour out His grace upon us when we seek to grow spiritually. As we consistently walk in the Spirit, we can experience true freedom in Christ. This kind of freedom allows us to be ourselves—unique, real, genuine—and to become all God has created us to be. Each of us can be free to be me!

Amazing grace! And He offers it freely to you and me. Are you experiencing this grace in your life? You can, you know, for it's up to you.

For Your Reflection

1. What was the most impressive Scripture verse or idea you experienced in studying this chapter?

2. Memorize the Scripture verse you identified above. If you did not select a verse, memorize Galatians 6:14.

3. Review the eight "our responsibility" ideas in a love-filled life (vv. 1-10). Write down one which needs improving in your own life.

4. What have you learned from this study of Galatians that can help you make progress in improving the idea you identified in number 3?

5. Write the first step you will take in making progress in improving that concept.

---

[1]Clifton J. Allen, general ed., *The Broadman Bible Commentary* (Nashville: Broadman Press, 1971), vol. 11, *2 Corinthians–Philemon* ("Galatians" by John William MacGorman), 121.

[2]Ibid., 124.

[3]Missionary George Trotter, conversation with writer, April 18, 1986.

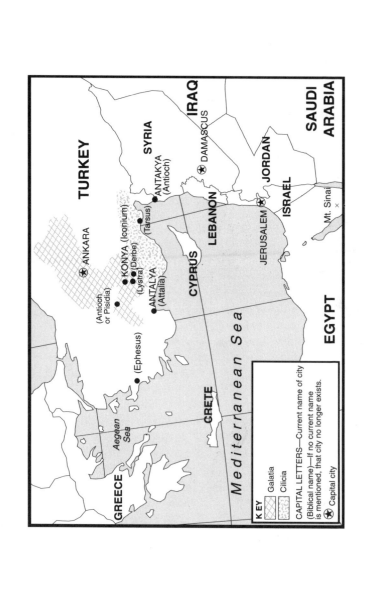

Outline of Ephesians

My Place in God's Purpose

Chapter 1—God's Purpose and Me
  I. God Created Me Special (1-14)
    A. A Saint—Who, Me? (1-2)
    B. Christ's Blessings Described (3-6)
      1. Spiritual—Not Material (3)
      2. Heavenly Experiences (3)
      3. Intentionally Chosen (4-6)
    C. Christ's Blessings Itemized (7-14)
      1. Redemption and Forgiveness (7)
      2. Wisdom and Understanding (8)
      3. God's Purpose Revealed (9-11)
      4. A Holy Heritage (12-13*a*)
      5. Gift of the Holy Spirit (13*b*-14)
  II. Model for a Leader's Prayer (15-23)
    A. Thanksgiving for Faithful Believers (15-16)
    B. Specific Prayers for Believers (17-23)
      1. Wisdom/Revelation to Know God Better (17)
      2. Eyes of the Heart Open to Know (18-23)
        a) God's Hope and Inheritance (18)
        b) Christ's Power (19-21)
        c) Relationship Between Christ and His Church (22-23)

Chapter 2—My Place as a New Creation
  I. Old Life Described (1-3)
  II. New Life Described (4-7)
  III. God's Plan for this New Life (8-10)
  IV. Oneness with All of God's Children (11-19)
    A. Extreme Differences Without Christ (11-12)
    B. Unity in Christ (13-19)
  V. Christ: My Cornerstone (20-22)

Chapter 3—Paul: A New Creation Prototype
   I. In Discerning the Mystery of God (1-6)
   II. In Receiving God's Grace (7-9)
   III. In Understanding God's Eternal Purpose for His Church (10-13)
   IV. In Prayer (14-21)
      A. A Position for Prayer (14)
      B. Specific Prayers for Us, the Church (15-19)
         1. That Our Hearts Will Be a Suitable Place in Which Christ Can Live (15-17*a*)
         2. That We Will Understand God's Love (17*b*-19*a*)
         3. That We Will Experience the Fullness of God (19*b*)
      C. Conclusion of the Prayer (20-21)

Chapter 4—My Place in God's Church
   I. Live Out the Christian Virtues (1)
      A. Humility and Gentleness (2*a*)
      B. Patience and Forbearance (2*b*)
   II. Keep Unity of the Spirit (3-6)
   III. Contribute to My Church's Growth (7-16)
      A. Acknowledge Gift of Grace in Every Member (7-10)
      B. Recognize God's Provision for Church Growth (11-13)
         1. God Gives Spiritual Gifts to Each Member (11)
         2. God Gives Gifts for a Purpose (12-13)
      C. Evaluate My Maturity (14-16)
         1. Stability in Doctrine (14)
         2. Speaking the Truth in Love (15)
         3. Faithfully Filling My Role in the Church (16)
   IV. Realize I Am Created to Be Like God (17-24)
      A. Break from My Past (17-19)
      B. Follow the Truths of Jesus (20-24)
   V. Live as a Christian—Not Just on Sundays (25-32)

Chapter 5—My Place in Marriage
   I. Live a Life of Love (1-2)
   II. Avoid Any Kind of Impurity (3-7)
   III. Live a Life of Light (8-14)
   IV. Be Filled with God's Spirit (15-20)
   V. Meet Each Other's Needs (21)
   VI. Understand Husband/Wife Roles in Marriage (22-33)
      A. Role of the Wife (22-24)
      B. Role of the Husband (25-33)

Chapter 6—My Place in Other Relationships

I. In My Family (1-4)

    A. Children and Parents (1-3)

    B. Parents and Children (4)

II. In the Workplace (5-9)

    A. Slaves and Masters (5-8)

    B. Masters and Slaves (9)

III. In My Victory over Satan (10-18)

    A. Know the Source of My Strength (10-11)

    B. Identify My Enemy (12)

    C. Dress for Combat (13-18)

        1. Put on the Whole Armor (13)

          a) Belt of Truth (14*a*)

          b) Breastplate of Righteousness (14*b*)

          c) Shoes of Readiness (15)

          d) Shield of Faith (16)

          e) Helmet of Salvation (17*a*)

          f) Sword of the Spirit (17*b*)

        2. Put on the Armor Through Prayer (18)

IV. In Praying for Missionaries and Other Leaders (19-20)

V. Conclusion (21-24)

Book of Ephesians

My Place in God's Purpose

A Word to the Reader

Do you find yourself among the numbers of women today who struggle to know their place in society? Many are looking for proven guidelines to determine their role in family and in the marketplace. You *can* know. The God Who made you and gifted you has a place for you not only in today's society but as a part of His eternal purpose. How comforting it is to realize that you not only *have* a place in God's purpose but that you can also *find* that place which ensures the highest quality of life! Finding your place in God's purpose will give direction and motivation to your life.

This study of Ephesians is designed to help you discover insights into God's purpose as well as your place in that purpose. Such discovery should result in spiritual growth. My prayer is that you will experience new depths of understanding of yourself and of God's purpose. And through understanding you will also experience great joy and fulfillment in who you are in God's eternal purpose.

You are about to begin the study of "the greatest piece of writing in all history," according to W. O. Carver, seminary professor who for 50 years made a serious study of this book.[1] Carver continues, "It is . . . the most comprehensive, the most complete, the most incisive and creative of all the New Testament writings."[2] As you study, open your heart, asking the Holy Spirit to guide and teach you. Determine that nothing will hinder your experiencing in full the awesome majesty of God found here.

Read slowly; seek to understand each word; invite each idea to penetrate your heart. Be honest with your thoughts and feelings. Be willing to obey God whatever He asks of you—for His glory. Mark the references to *grace* throughout these chapters as you praise God for His grace at work in your life. At the close of each chapter, you will find questions to aid you in reflecting upon what you have learned.

Introduction to the Book

Ephesians takes its name from the people living in Ephesus. Located in western Turkey, Ephesus was the capital city of the Roman province of Asia in Paul's time (see p. 54). Strategically located three miles from the sea, Ephesus was the junction for trade from both east and west.

In addition, this cosmopolitan commercial center was the location of one of the seven wonders of the ancient world: Temple of Diana (Artemis) where prostitution was legal. Silversmiths made profits from selling statuettes of this fertility goddess.[3]

A survey of additional biblical references to Ephesus helps to broaden one's understanding of the church established there and its people.

1. Acts 18:18-21—Paul establishes the church in Ephesus, leaving his helpers, Priscilla and Aquila, to disciple the group of believers.
2. Acts 19—Paul disciples believers in Ephesus for two years (vv. 1-21). Later a riot erupts among silversmiths when individuals turn to Christ.
3. Acts 20:13-38—Paul and elders from the church at Ephesus experience a moving farewell.
4. Revelation 2:1-7—God gives a message to the Ephesian church: "You have forsaken your first love" (Rev. 2:4*b*).

While the book of Ephesians is addressed to "the saints in Ephesus," Curtis Vaughan notes, "These words . . . though found in the great majority of the Greek manuscripts, are not supported by the oldest and best manuscripts of this letter. It appears that Ephesians was originally a circular letter . . . and intended for all the churches of the Roman province of Asia (of which Ephesus was the capital city)."[4] Absence of Paul's personal greeting and reference to individuals within the church lends credence to its being a circular letter.

Ephesians begins with the name Paul, indicating he is the writer. Paul (Roman name) is the same person as Saul (Jewish name) who experienced a life-changing encounter with Jesus enroute to Damascus to persecute the Christians (Acts 9:1-19).

This letter, more correctly called a treatise, was probably written during Paul's first imprisonment in Rome in the early part of the sixties A.D.[5] Notice three references in Ephesians to Paul's being in prison: (1) "For this reason I, Paul, the prisoner of Christ Jesus" (Eph. 3:1); (2) "As a prisoner for the Lord, then" (Eph. 4:1); (3) "For which I am an ambassador in chains" (Eph. 6:20).

Various themes have been identified for Ephesians. One of the most comprehensive ones, by Vaughan, is "the eternal purpose of God and the place of Christ and His people in that purpose."[6] This statement forms the backdrop for this commentary. I stand amazed at how relevant Ephesians, written almost 2,000 years ago, is for women today! May God's Spirit enable each of us to find our place in His purpose.

[1] W. O. Carver, *Ephesians: The Glory of God in the Christian Calling* (1949; reprint, Nashville: Broadman Press, 1979), 7.

[2] Ibid., 18.

[3] Madeleine S. Miller and J. Lane Miller, *Harper's Bible Dictionary* (New York: Harper and Brothers, Publishers, 1956), 136 and 167.

[4] Curtis Vaughan, *Ephesians, A Study Guide Commentary* (Grand Rapids: Zondervan Publishing House, 1977), 14.

[5] Clifton J. Allen, general ed., The Broadman Bible Commentary (Nashville: Broadman Press, 1971), vol. 11, *2 Corinthians–Philemon* ("Ephesians" by Ralph P. Martin), 128.

[6] Vaughan, *Ephesians,* 12.

1. God's Purpose and Me

I. God Created Me Special (1-14)
A. A Saint—Who, Me? (1-2)

"Paul, an apostle of Christ Jesus by the will of God, to the saints in Ephesus, the faithful in Christ Jesus: Grace and peace to you from God our Father and the Lord Jesus Christ" (Eph. 1:1-2).

This letter was written to the saints at Ephesus, and because we know God's Word speaks to us today, this letter is written to us also. Me, a saint?

A first reaction is No! We feel ourselves to be far from sainthood and the goodness that implies, such as is seen in the life of Mother Teresa of India. However, a closer look at the meaning of the word *saint* reveals that saints in the New Testament were "all Christians."[1] If we are believers in Jesus Christ ("faithful in Christ Jesus"), then we are saints. We may not be perfect saints, but we *are* saints.

Paul identifies himself as an apostle. Vaughan clarifies, "In the New Testament, the word *apostle* regularly denotes a person engaged by another to carry out a commission."[2] Paul felt that being an apostle was God's will for his life. Jesus Himself was called an apostle (Heb. 3:1); that is, sent from God to carry out a commission.

Grace and peace is a favorite couplet of Paul which he uses to wish for the saints God's undeserved favor (grace) and a God-given calm deep within (peace)—not just the absence from strife. As saints (believers) today, we can be recipients of God's favor and His calm deep within us.

B. Christ's Blessings Described (3-6)

"Praise be to the God and Father of our Lord Jesus Christ, who has blessed us in the heavenly realms with every spiritual blessing in Christ. For he chose us in him before the creation of the world to be holy and blameless in his sight. In love he predestined us to be adopted as his sons through Jesus Christ, in accordance with his pleasure and will—to the praise of his glorious grace, which he has freely given us in the One he loves" (Eph. 1:3-6).

Paul describes three blessings which come from Christ: (1) spiritual blessings; (2) "heavenly" experiences; and (3) intentionally chosen.

1. Spiritual—Not Material (3)

God has not promised us material blessings, but He has promised *every*—not just *one*—spiritual blessing in Christ. Such knowledge causes Paul to praise God.

2. Heavenly Experiences (3)

Notice four additional references in Ephesians to "heavenly realms": (1) 1:20—where Jesus is now; (2) 2:6—where believers have fellowship with Christ; (3) 3:10—where heavenly powers learn the wisdom of God shown through His people; and (4) 6:12—spiritual warfare where believers confront forces of evil.

We are reminded that we Christians are citizens of two kingdoms: spiritual and earthly. We are to live out our daily lives conscious of our blessings as well as responsibilities in each.

3. Intentionally Chosen (4-6)

Chose[n] and *predestined* (vv. 4-5), two key words, are the basis for these blessings.

Chosen. As a child, did you ever want to play a game in which you were last to be chosen? That is an awful feeling. But as a believer in Christ, you were chosen by God even before the world was created. Vaughan explains that "God has chosen Christians to be His people, to be the means of carrying out His purpose in this world."[3]

What a wonderful thought it is to realize we are not only chosen by God, but that He wants to use us in helping Him carry out His purpose in the world! We are to be holy (separated)—and blameless—"the Christian standard is nothing less than perfection."[4]

Predestined is the second important word in this passage (v. 5). Webster's meaning is "to determine, or settle, beforehand." In many ways *predestined* and *chosen* are alike. Theologians refer to this concept as the doctrine (teaching) of election. This is "an act of choice whereby God selects an individual or group out of a larger company for a purpose or destiny that He appoints."[5]

The doctrine of election has its roots in the Old Testament. For example: Abraham was chosen to leave his home country; Isaac was chosen rather than Ishmael; and Israel was chosen over other nations. Each was chosen to be a channel through which others would be blessed.

Notice all of this is done in love (v. 5). We are even adopted as children of God through Jesus Christ—all in accordance with His will. Our hearts join with Paul's in bursting forth in praise for God's grace. We are special, chosen by God to help Him carry out His purpose. Wow!

Paul continues as he itemizes five blessings received from Christ.

C. Christ's Blessings Itemized (7-14)
1. Redemption and Forgiveness (7)

"In him we have redemption through his blood, the forgiveness of sins, in accordance with the riches of God's grace" (Eph. 1:7).

As Christians, you and I have been redeemed, that is, delivered from sin through Christ's sacrificial death on the Cross. And as a part of that redemption we have received forgiveness of sins when we have repented of those sins. We continue to receive forgiveness as we repent of sins and ask for God's cleansing (1 John 1:9). This is not the result of anything we do; it's only God's grace.

2. Wisdom and Understanding (8)

"That he lavished on us with all wisdom and understanding" (Eph. 1:8).

Wisdom means having insight to use knowledge in an appropriate manner. Understanding means the ability to grasp the meaning of a truth. God has lavished upon us as Christians these abilities.

3. God's Purpose Revealed (9-11)

"And he made known to us the mystery of his will according to his good pleasure, which he purposed in Christ, to be put into effect when the times will have reached their fulfillment—to bring all things in heaven and on earth together under one head, even Christ. In him we were also chosen, having been predestined according to the plan of him who works out everything in conformity with the purpose of his will" (Eph. 1:9-11).

How privileged we are! While God's purpose is still a mystery to unbelievers, we who believe in Jesus can understand God's purpose. And what is His purpose? God's purpose is to bring together all things in heaven and earth under the headship of Christ in the proper time ("when the times will have reached their fulfillment"—v. 10). One day there will be no more wars among nations, no natural disasters, no violence, no hunger, no discord among peoples of the world. *All* will be brought together in unity under Jesus' leadership. What a wonderful day that will be!

You and I—as are all believers—are chosen to be a part of God's master plan. We are not isolated individuals struggling through life without purpose and meaning. We are chosen! We are chosen by God through Christ to share His kind of love with all peoples who could also find their place in God's purpose.

Such knowledge is almost too much for us! Why are we so favored? Paul lists another blessing.

4. A Holy Heritage (12-13*a*)

"In order that we, who were the first to hope in Christ, might be for the praise of his glory. And you also were included in Christ when you heard the word of truth, the gospel of your salvation" (Eph. 1:12-13a).

We are saved so that our lives might bring glory to God. *Glory* means "splendor of a very high degree; also used of those qualities or facts which cause the splendor."[6]

Our heritage includes believers who have set a good example with their lives in bringing glory to God. The phrase "first to hope in Christ" refers to Jews while the phrase "and you also were included" refers to Gentiles.

Christian women of today, we have the great heritage of both Jews and Gentiles whose lives have glorified God. In learning from them, may we too join those whose greatest desire is to glorify God. We have a holy heritage.

5. Gift of the Holy Spirit (13*b*-14)

"Having believed, you were marked in him with a seal, the promised Holy Spirit, who is a deposit guaranteeing our inheritance until the redemption of those who are God's possession—to the praise of his glory" (Eph. 1:13b-14).

Recently, my husband and I put a deposit down on some furniture we were buying. This deposit was a pledge that we would pay the full amount in the future and receive all the furniture we had originally selected.

Paul writes that the Holy Spirit is the deposit, or promise, to us that one day in the future we will receive our full inheritance—living with Jesus for eternity. God is gracious in giving us the Holy Spirit, Who comes to live within us as we open our hearts to Jesus. As wonderful a gift as He is, the Holy Spirit is just a deposit of the enormous inheritance we will receive some day in heaven. Such knowledge leads us to want to praise God as did Paul in Ephesians. And Paul, overcome with awe from God's goodness, was moved to pray.

Prayer, talking to and listening to God, is one of the most important things—if not *the* most important—a believer can do. Paul prays for his fellow Christians. This leader's prayer is worthy of our study.

II. Model for a Leader's Prayer (15-23)

A. Thanksgiving for Faithful Believers (15-16)

"For this reason, ever since I heard about your faith in the Lord Jesus and your love for all the saints, I have not stopped giving thanks for you, remembering you in my prayers" (Eph. 1:15-16).

Paul consistently thanks God for the Ephesians and remembers to pray for them. How encouraging this must have been to them! His prayer was prompted by what he had heard of God's grace at work in their hearts ("for this reason"), the faith they had in Jesus as well as their sacrificial love (agape) for fellow believers.

If you are a leader in your church or a parent in your home, are you praying for those under your responsibility? Are you encouraging them because of what you see Christ doing in their lives? Paul's prayer can be a model for us. He continues with specific prayers.

B. Specific Prayers for Believers (17-23)
1. Wisdom/Revelation to Know God Better (17)
"I keep asking that the God of our Lord Jesus Christ, the glorious Father, may give you the Spirit of wisdom and revelation, so that you may know him better" (Eph. 1:17).

A rustic wooden plaque on my desk carrying the words "That I may know Him" has been an inspiration and challenge to me since college days. My campus minister burned that key verse into a small slab from a tree felled by a Mississippi tornado which uprooted large numbers of trees on our campus. Students slept untouched by the violent storm.

That night we experienced God's protecting care. My desire was heightened to have the wisdom to know Him better each day of my life. Could this be your desire also?

2. Eyes of the Heart Open to Know (18-23)
Paul continues to pray, asking that the eyes of our heart be open to know three different ideas. The phrase, "eyes of your heart," refers to the whole person, every part of the being. First, Paul prays that our heart eyes be open to:

a) God's Hope and Inheritance (18)
"I pray also that the eyes of your heart may be enlightened in order that you may know the hope to which he has called you, the riches of his glorious inheritance in the saints" (Eph. 1:18).

Millions of people in our world today are without hope. But when Jesus comes into the life of a believer, that person has a whole new outlook on life, for she is called by God to become a child of the King and to take a rightful place in helping His kingdom come on earth.

While there are several views about interpreting "his glorious inheritance," most writers agree this refers to believers' knowing how special they are in the sight of God. Paul asks God to open our heart eyes to a second idea:

b) Christ's Power (19-21)
"And his incomparably great power for us who believe. That power is like the working of his mighty strength, which he exerted in Christ when he raised him from the dead and seated him at his right hand in the heavenly realms, far above all rule and authority, power and dominion, and every title that can be given, not only in the present age but also in the one to come" (Eph. 1:19-21).

Paul wants us to know God's "incomparably great power." The word *power* comes from the Greek word *dunamis,* from which we have the word *dynamite.*

In 1993 terrorists in the United States used dynamite to seriously damage New York's World Trade Center. A few weeks later terrorists in Italy used dynamite again to destroy the large part of one wing of the world-famous Uffizi Gallery in Florence, Italy. Dynamite is powerful. But the power of God which Paul describes here makes these terrorist acts pale in comparison.

God's power is (1) the kind God exercised when He raised Christ from the dead and (2) the kind He used to seat Christ at His right hand in heaven (v. 20).

Can we grasp the impact of Paul's prayer? Our minds must stretch beyond *Star Wars* and anything one could imagine. Paul asks God to help all believers, including you and me today, to know the kind of power He exercised in raising Jesus from the dead and to live with Him in heaven.

But there's more! Because He lives we too shall live! (1 Thess. 4:13-18). God's power is available today to raise us from the dead to live with Jesus eternally. God's power is available today to change lives. That same power is available now to help us overcome any obstacle of life. Vaughan writes, "The power available to us in daily living is not to be conceived of as a tiny brook, barely meeting the demands made on it. It is like a surging river, driving before itself all the obstacles it may encounter."[7]

In the latter part of this verse Paul assures us that Christ's position is greater than any being in heaven or on earth. And to think, He's our Saviour!

Paul again asks that the heart eyes be open to:

c) Relationship Between Christ and His Church (22-23)

"And God placed all things under his feet and appointed him to be head over everything for the church, which is his body, the fulness of him who fills everything in every way" (Eph. 1:22-23).

Jesus is the head of the church. The church, made up of believers in Jesus, is the body. As head of the church, Jesus has ultimate authority over the believers. The head-body relationship implies there is a vital union between believers and Jesus (see John 15:5). As believers look to Him, the Head, they can be filled with His Spirit.

The purpose of God is to bring unity into His world. He sent His Son, Jesus, into the world to reconcile every person with Himself. Because Jesus died for our sins and was raised again, He is worthy to reconcile every person in the world to God. "I am the way and the truth and the life. No one comes to the Father except through me" (John 14:6).

As a part of His body, we have the privilege of being His feet, His hands, His heart, His love in a world which still desperately needs to be unified in Christ. If God's purpose is to bring unity in the world through Christ, and if we believers are a part of Christ's body (the church), is your life's plan in God's purpose beginning to become clearer? Search for additional insights as you continue your study of Ephesians. Sheila West in *Beyond Chaos* writes, "Being God's woman in God's plan is not a price to pay, but a priority to cherish."[8]

For Your Reflection

1. What idea or Scripture verse in this study has impressed you most?

2. Memorize your selected Scripture verse or Ephesians 1:11.

3. Write your interpretation, based on this study, of

   A. God's purpose:

   B. Your place in God's plan:

4. Write two or three sentences of praise to God for what He has done for you.

---

[1] Madeleine S. Miller and J. Lane Miller, *Harper's Bible Dictionary* (New York: Harper and Brothers, Publishers, 1956), 635.

[2] Curtis Vaughan, *Ephesians, A Study Guide Commentary* (Grand Rapids: Zondervan Publishing House, 1977), 13.

[3] Ibid., 20.

[4] William Barclay, *The Letters to the Galatians and Ephesians,* The Daily Study Bible Series, rev. ed. (Edinburgh: Saint Andrew Press, 1983), 79.

[5] Vaughan, *Ephesians,* 20.

[6] Miller and Miller, *Harper's Bible Dictionary,* 228.

[7] Vaughan, *Ephesians,* 37.

[8] Sheila West, *Beyond Chaos* (Colorado Springs: NavPress, 1991), 35.

2. My Place as a New Creation

What woman is not interested in a new creation? We may think more about *owning* a new creation than *being* a new creation, however. How can we become a new creation? God has that power to transform us. New always implies old, and the life before one becomes a Christian is described at the very beginning of this chapter.

I. Old Life Described (1-3)

"As for you, you were dead in your transgressions and sins, in which you used to live when you followed the ways of this world and of the ruler of the kingdom of the air, the spirit who is now at work in those who are disobedient. All of us also lived among them at one time, gratifying the cravings of our sinful nature and following its desires and thoughts. Like the rest, we were by nature objects of wrath" (Eph. 2:1-3).

Dead or death means separation from loved ones and friends. When a person is spiritually dead, she is separated eternally from God. Spiritual death occurs when a woman is involved in transgressions and sins. The word *transgressions* means "losing one's way or straying from the right road" while *sins* means "missing the mark."[1]

Think about it. Have we achieved the goal God has set for our lives? Are we *being* and *doing* what God wants of us? Are our lives making the highest contribution possible to God's kingdom? If not, we are missing the mark—*sin.*

In Romans 3:23 Paul writes, "For all have sinned and fall short of the glory of God." This means we live to please ourselves. We cannot understand people who give their lives in service as do, for example, missionaries. We pursue whatever we crave or desire. All of us have lived to satisfy our own sinful natures. Sin dulls our senses. Moral decay sets in. Sin places blinders on our eyes so that we do not see the spiritual things of God.

The old life we lived is governed by dictates of the "ruler of the kingdom of the air." I remember my visit many years ago to Thailand as if it was last week. In Bangkok, the capital city, I saw on almost every corner spirit

71

houses with bowls of food being offered to their gods. A heavy, oppressive, cloud-like sinister feeling hung over that city—ruled by the kingdom of the air. Unfortunately, this situation is not confined to Thailand, whose state religion is Buddhism, but can be felt around the world.

The ruler of the air, Satan, seeks to influence you and me. When we sin, we are never quite the same again even though we may seek and find forgiveness. Just as extracting a nail from wood mars that piece of wood, so sin leaves its marks on our lives. Sin in any form makes us objects of God's wrath. Some may think of God only as a God of love. He is that, but the reverse side is wrath. To be righteous, God must be both love and wrath. When we have refused God's love, we receive His wrath. How do we escape His wrath?

II. New Life Described (4-7)

"But because of his great love for us, God, who is rich in mercy, made us alive with Christ even when we were dead in transgressions—it is by grace you have been saved. And God raised us up with Christ and seated us with him in the heavenly realms in Christ Jesus, in order that in the coming ages he might show the incomparable riches of his grace, expressed in his kindness to us in Christ Jesus" (Eph. 2:4-7).

How thankful I am for that little word *but*, which indicates some kind of change is occurring! We don't have to stay dead in sin, blind to spiritual truths, or separated from God. Merciful God loved us so much that He made a way out for us to be alive with Christ. What love! Alive! How glorious!

Many of us have anxiously awaited the results of a physical examination. When the doctor said, "Benign," we have experienced not only a tremendous relief but also a new lease on life. Alive!

Our merciful God has loved us so much that He has provided a way for us to move from spiritual death to spiritual life. Nothing we do can bring this about; it is the result only of God's grace—His unmerited favor. Spiritual aliveness ensures that we will be raised to sit with Christ in heavenly places and show God's amazing grace in the coming ages. Are we sure we know the way God has provided and are experiencing it? How are we saved?

III. God's Plan for this New Life (8-10)

"For it is by grace you have been saved, through faith—and this not from yourselves, it is the gift of God—not by works, so that no one can boast. For we are God's workmanship, created in Christ Jesus to do good works, which God prepared in advance for us to do" (Eph 2:8-10).

Paul writes to the Corinthians that "God made him [Jesus] who had no sin to be sin for us, so that in him we might become the righteousness of God" (2 Cor. 5:21). God's grace in action! To think that we can become the righteousness of God—"conformity to the character of God."[2] And it

Ex 33:13

is by this grace we are saved from the old life to the new. Such a change comes only through accepting Jesus as Saviour, which is often described as a new birth.

This is true for the most sophisticated as well as for the most uneducated person. These verses may well be the most important ones in the entire book. Let's look at the meaning of three pivotal words appearing here: *grace, saved, faith.*

Grace—God's favor which is not deserved. God initiated this; we are only recipients of His meeting our needs.

Saved—Rescued from danger. When we are unsaved, not only are we headed toward eternal damnation but we are missing the quality of life which ensures the best in the world in which we live.

Faith—Active trust, based on the promises of God. Our younger son, John, became very much interested in "making a decision" soon after David, his older brother, had made public his decision to trust Jesus as his Saviour. I asked David to share with his brother the meaning of *believe* (trust).

Climbing up the ladder to the top bunk, David replied, "It's like this. I'm climbing up this ladder, and I know it's going to hold me up. That's the way it is with Jesus. You can count on Him."

In his childlike way, David illustrated what it means for one to have faith.

We are *saved,* rescued from eternal danger—eternal separation from God—to eternal presence with God. We are saved not because we are good or have done great deeds, but only by God's *grace.* Even if it were possible for us to work to save ourselves (and we cannot), we might boast about our ability. We become saved when we place our *faith,* our trust, in God and His provision for our salvation through Jesus Christ.

Someone has described *trust* as putting all of one's weight down on an object. We are assured that the object of our faith, Christ Jesus, is Who God says He is—His Son, love gift to the world, and the way through which we are no longer separated from God. We can put all our weight on this assurance.

Jesus died on the Cross to become the substitute for us in our old sinful nature. We agree with God our old life is wrong; in sorrow we turn from that old life and embrace God's provision through Christ. Now we are no longer separated from God, but acceptance of Jesus as our personal Saviour restores our formerly broken relationship with God.

"Made by God" ("we are God's workmanship"—v. 10), Paul writes that we are made to do good works which God has planned for us to do. Not only are we saved but we are saved to do something. What a privilege! The eternal Creator's plan has a place for you and me. We are not to aimlessly wander through this life, but to find and follow God's purpose for our lives. What an adventure! How many people live their whole lives without attempting to discover their place in God's purpose?

Deborah is a young adult who *has* discovered her place in God's purpose. She says she is a firstborn: "classic melancholy, overachieving perfectionist whose basic nature is painfully shy, insecure, and easily intimidated by people."[3]

How in the world, then, did she ever achieve her present position as vice-president for ACTS and FamilyNet, two Christian television networks?

Success has come in her saying yes to God. But those responses have not always been easy in spite of her early acceptance of Christ and growing up in a Christian home. In college God spoke to her through Jeremiah 29:11: "'For I know the plans I have for you,' declares the Lord, 'plans to prosper you and not to harm you, plans to give you hope and a future.'" At that time she made the commitment to follow God's goals for her life rather than her self-appointed ones.

Deborah had wanted to become an actress in New York; instead, God led her to a seminary. She did not want to be single until she was 35, but God led her to wait through singleness and celibacy. And by waiting on Him, she knows God gave her a husband who even surpassed her wishes and dreams. She did not want to go to the Christian television networks, but by following God's leadership she faithfully worked there over nine years before being offered her present role.

Today Deborah testifies, "Whatever success you see is the grace and handiwork of God in the life of an insecure, timid, ordinary girl, who believes she can do nothing apart from God; and whose loving, godly parents taught her to cling to His promise that 'I can do all things through Christ who strengthens me.'"[4] Deborah: a modern-day example of God's workmanship—made to do good works.

Women of today, you and I are saved not by our works but to do good works. We too should be involved in helping the poor, the hungry around the world, the homeless, the friendless, the sick—all who need a caring touch from a follower of Jesus, Who "did not come to be served, but to serve, and to give his life as a ransom for many" (Mark 10:45).

IV. Oneness with All God's Children (11-19)

Earlier we noted that God's purpose in the world was to bring about unity among all people. When Christ enters a person's heart, cultural barriers can begin to disappear no matter how wide the differences. Such unity is not easy or possible in our own strength, but only in Christ's. Members of the early church struggled with achieving unity.

A. Extreme Differences Without Christ (11-12)

"Therefore, remember that formerly you who are Gentiles by birth and called 'uncircumcised' by those who call themselves 'the circumcision' (that done in the body by the hands of men)—remember that at that time you were separate

74

from Christ, excluded from citizenship in Israel and foreigners to the covenants of the promise, without hope and without God in the world" (Eph. 2:11-12).

Jews felt that individuals must be circumcised before becoming Christians (for discussion on "circumcised" see pp. 37-39).

Those of us who live in the twentieth century can hardly grasp the contempt with which Jews held Gentiles (non-Jews). "It was not even lawful to render help to a Gentile woman in childbirth, for that would be to bring another Gentile into the world. The barrier between Jew and Gentile was absolute."[5]

Notice in verse 12 the condition of the Gentiles: *Exclude*

(1) Separate from Christ—Through the ages they could not look forward to a Messiah as did the Jews;

(2) Excluded from citizenship in Israel—Gentiles had no part in the Israelite nation where God's reign took an earthly form;

(3) Foreigners to the covenants of the promise—The promise to Abraham (Gen. 12:1-3) was often renewed, but only to the Jews;

(4) Without hope—When a Gentile loved one died, there was no hope of seeing him again in eternity;

(5) Without God in the world—Not have a personal relationship with the eternal God to guide them in the darkness of this world.

The picture was bleak. However, the words *but now* in verse 13 signify change.

B. Unity in Christ (13-19)

"But now in Christ Jesus you who once were far away have been brought near through the blood of Christ.

"For He Himself is our peace, who has made the two one and has destroyed the barrier, the dividing wall of hostility, by abolishing in his flesh the law with its commandments and regulations. His purpose was to create in himself one new man out of the two, thus making peace, and in this one body to reconcile both of them to God through the cross, by which he put to death their hostility. He came and preached peace to you who were far away and peace to those who were near. For through him we both have access to the Father by one Spirit.

"Consequently, you are no longer foreigners and aliens, but fellow citizens with God's people and members of God's household" (Eph. 2:13-19).

Through the death of Jesus on the Cross, barriers were destroyed between Gentiles and Jews, these two groups representing "the two hostile sections of humanity."[6] "The dividing wall of hostility" refers to the whole Mosaic law, an elaborate legal system with very tiny regulations.

Now every person, regardless of his background, had direct access to God through Jesus ("brought near" in v. 13). Notice that Paul did not say Christ *brings* peace, but that He *is* our peace. Only through Christ can barriers and walls of hostility and unnecessary regulations be dissolved, allowing people to experience true unity.

Not only did God bring Jew and Gentile together but He created a new man from those reconciled to Himself through Christ. Prophets from the Old Testament foretold this newness as early as 500 years before Christ was born.[7] Ezekiel wrote: "I will give you a new heart and put a new spirit in you" (36:26a). And Isaiah, probably greatest of the Hebrew prophets, penned, "You will be called by a new name" (62:2).

In numerous countries throughout the world today when an individual becomes a Christian, she is given a new name—a Christian name—to denote the change which has taken place in her heart and life.

With reconciliation comes citizenship, and even more: all God's children are united as members of God's household. Not only is there unity in the legal world (citizenship) but also unity comes in the warmth of fellowship with other believers and intimacy with God through Jesus. If this could happen in the early church, could it not happen in our world today? "For nothing is impossible with God" (Luke 1:37). Are you and I actively seeking our place in helping God's purpose become a reality now?

V. Christ: My Cornerstone (20-22)

"Built on the foundation of the apostles and prophets, with Christ Jesus himself as the chief cornerstone. In him the whole building is joined together and rises to become a holy temple in the Lord. And in him you too are being built together to become a dwelling in which God lives by his Spirit" (Eph. 2:20-22).

Paul changes his writing to describe a building, but what a building! First he mentions it is built on the foundation of the apostles of the New Testament and the prophets from the Old. Carver interprets this as "the foundation taught, and by their teaching laid down for us all, by the apostles and prophets."[8] But who occupies the place of the chief cornerstone? None other than Christ Jesus Himself. He is the One on Whom the entire structure depends.

All Christians, regardless of race or status in life, are joined together in forming one great temple, or church, in Jesus—a living organism.

Notice Paul's closing words of this chapter as he reminds us that we too are a part of this building with Christ as our foundation. Storms of life may come, but with Christ as our chief cornerstone, we can withstand any onslaught.

With reverence and awe we read that God lives by His Spirit within us. Paul shares a similar idea with the Christian in Corinth: "Do you not know that your body is a temple of the Holy Spirit, who is in you, whom you have received from God? You are not your own" (1 Cor. 6:19).

Women of today, when we grasp these concepts, there comes to us a consciousness of barriers in our world today which can be broken down as individuals become reconciled to God through Jesus. What are we doing within God's purpose to help to bring down such barriers as racial, economic, social, educational, and between factions which may exsist in our churches or even in our women's work?

Also there comes to us an understanding of the sacredness of life and a deeper awareness of the necessity for our taking good care of our bodies which house God's Spirit. We have become a new creation. And we are just one part of God's new creations throughout the earth forming one colossal spiritual Temple for the glory of God. Hallelujah!

For Your Reflection

1. Complete the chart by writing in words which describe your life in each category.

Old Life	New Life

2. What person or circumstance did God use to bring you to the point of accepting Jesus as your personal Saviour?

   Thank God for Jesus your Saviour and also for the person/circumstance God used to help you.

3. If you are not a member of a church, ask God to guide you to one in which you can bring others to Jesus and His church.

4. Write Ephesians 2:8-9. Commit these verses to memory.

[1]Curtis Vaughan, *Ephesians, A Study Guide Commentary* (Grand Rapids: Zondervan Publishing House, 1977), 44.

[2]Tommy Lea, New Testament professor, Southwestern Baptist Theological Seminary, in sermon at Travis Avenue Baptist Church, Fort Worth, Texas, August 8, 1993.

[3]Deborah Key, testimony at Travis Avenue Baptist Church, Fort Worth, Texas, July 18, 1993.

[4]Ibid.

[5]William Barclay, *The Letters to the Galatians and Ephesians,* The Daily Study Bible Series, rev. ed. (Edinburgh: Saint Andrew Press, 1983), 107.

[6]Vaughan, *Ephesians,* 58.

[7]Madeleine S. Miller and J. Lane Miller, *Harper's Bible Dictionary* (New York: Harper and Brothers, Publishers, 1956), 181 and 285.

[8]W. O. Carver, *Ephesians: The Glory of God in the Christian Calling* (1949; reprint, Nashville: Broadman Press, 1979), 98.

3. Paul: A New Creation Prototype

A prototype, according to Webster, is "an original model on which something is patterned." Chapter 2 emphasized "My Place as a New Creation." In this chapter we see a close-up of Paul, "an original model" of a new creation in Christ. While not the first Christian, Paul can serve as a pattern for our lives today.

I. In Discerning the Mystery of God (1-6)

"For this reason I, Paul, the prisoner of Christ Jesus for the sake of you Gentiles—surely you have heard about the administration of God's grace that was given to me for you, that is, the mystery made known to me by revelation, as I have already written briefly. In reading this, then, you will be able to understand my insight into the mystery of Christ, which was not made known to men in other generations as it has now been revealed by the Spirit to God's holy apostles and prophets. This mystery is that through the gospel the Gentiles are heirs together with Israel, members together of one body, and sharers together in the promise in Christ Jesus" (Eph. 3:1-6).

The first three words of the first verse connect us with the last idea in the previous chapter in which we discovered Christ as the cornerstone of our lives. Paul acknowledges he is literally a prisoner because of his ministry to the Gentiles. At the end of this first verse Paul seems to break his thought, not resuming it again until verse 14.

Three times Paul refers to "the mystery": "Mystery made known to me by revelation" (v. 3); "you will be able to understand my insight into the mystery of Christ" (v. 4); and "This mystery is" (v. 6). The term *mystery religions* was very popular in Paul's day. Leaders in groups of mystery religions communicated their deepest truths only to their followers through special initiation ceremonies. No one else was privileged to have this information.

We stand on tiptoes in anticipation of peering into the very heart of God to understand the mystery to which Paul refers in this chapter. Our womanly curiosity prompts us to probe the meaning of the word *mystery* (v. 6). The meaning is that through Jesus, Gentiles are (1) "heirs together with Israel"; (2) "members together of one body"; and (3) "sharers together in the promise in Christ Jesus."

Notice the use of the word *together* in each phrase. Jews and Gentiles are to be together in Christ. As we have seen in Ephesians 2:14, Jesus "has destroyed the barrier, the dividing wall of hostility" between Jew and non-Jew. God's original purpose of unity is now being more closely realized.

Such information may not seem to be a mystery to us today, for we know that God gave His Son Jesus so that peoples of all races might have eternal life. But such understanding has not always been widespread. "Knowledge of God did not come all at once. God worked through history to reveal His will as people were prepared to accept it."[1]

In Old Testament days God was preparing His people for the birth of Jesus. As Jesus entered into His mission on earth, He gathered 12 disciples around Him, who became missionaries. While they preached first only to Jews, eventually the disciples grasped the purpose for Jesus' life, death, and resurrection. The Apostle Paul, while not one of the 12 disciples, made an unusual contribution through his ministry in helping individuals understand Christ had come to save Gentiles as well as Jews. Up until this time, this truth had not been made clear. What a glorious revelation! No one is excluded from God's love if he only will avail himself of the opportunity to accept Jesus as his Saviour.

Women of today, as believers in Jesus, let us follow Paul's example in discerning the mystery of God. Let us take advantage of every opportunity, personally as well as in supporting others, to share Jesus not with just "our kind of people," but with all kinds so that God's mystery can be clearly understood in our homes, communities, and world.

II. In Receiving God's Grace (7-9)

"I became a servant of this gospel by the gift of God's grace given me through the working of his power. Although I am less than the least of all God's people, this grace was given me: To preach to the Gentiles the unsearchable riches of Christ and to make plain to everyone the administration of this mystery, which for ages past was kept hidden in God, who created all things" (Eph. 3:7-9).

Paul grew up with every advantage as a Jew. Having studied with some of the great Jewish leaders, he was soon to become an outstanding Pharisee. In fact, he was enroute to Damascus to kill all Christians when he had an encounter with the Living Lord (Acts 9). Through God's grace, undeserved and unexpected love, Paul came to accept Jesus as his Saviour and Lord and soon began to minister to the very Christians he had previously planned to persecute. Such a transformation could happen only by God's grace.

The Apostle registers his utter unworthiness in being forgiven and chosen by God. He realizes this grace was given to him for a purpose, which is twofold. First, to preach to the Gentiles the riches of Christ. Those riches are so great they are beyond anyone's imagination. The second facet of that purpose is to make plain the mystery of the gospel: Jesus came to save all peoples.

Women of today, Paul is an example of God's grace. As you and I have placed our trust in Jesus, we too are recipients of that same grace. Paul realized God extended His grace to him for a two-pronged purpose. Have we fully grasped that God's grace has been given to us also for this twofold purpose—(1) sharing with all kinds of people the abundant life Christ offers and (2) in every way possible help share Jesus with all people of the entire world?

III. In Understanding God's Eternal Purpose for His Church (10-13)

"His intent was that now, through the church, the manifold wisdom of God should be made known to the rulers and authorities in the heavenly realms, according to his eternal purpose which he accomplished in Christ Jesus our Lord. In him and through faith in him we may approach God with freedom and confidence. I ask you, therefore, not to be discouraged because of my sufferings for you, which are your glory" (Eph. 3:10-13).

Recognizing God's purpose in giving His grace, Paul moves from his individual responsibility to that of the church. He "provided the church with drive and vision fuelled by a sense of urgency, derived from his conviction that the Last Days and the return of Jesus as Messiah were approaching."[2]

In verse 10 notice the church is to make known the "manifold wisdom of God." *Manifold* means "marked by diversity or variety." God's wisdom is so varied that it can match any need. Nevertheless, we have the responsibility—the privilege—to make His wisdom clear to our generation.

Paul mentions in this same verse the target group to which the church should make known the diverse wisdom of God: "Rulers and authorities in the heavenly realms" (v. 10). Even the angels are interested in such revelation (1 Peter 1:12). As a part of His church, we are to share Jesus with all people of the world in such a way that those in heavenly realms will be aware of what the body (church) is doing. This is a part of God's eternal purpose accomplished through His Son, Jesus.

The Apostle reminds us through Jesus we may approach God freely and with all confidence "so that we can receive mercy and find grace to help us in our time of need" (Heb. 4:16). But there are millions of people in our world who cannot experience this freedom. They know God only as a God of fear and wrath. They simply do not know He loves them and has given Jesus through Whom they can freely and boldly approach Him. Thousands of missionaries throughout the world are sharing Christ with unsaved people.

Still, countless people die daily without knowing Jesus personally as their Saviour because they have either turned a deaf ear to the missionary or they live in a part of the world where missionaries are not allowed to go. More people willing to cross cultural barriers are needed to tell them the gospel.

The church today has the glorious privilege of telling the good news of Jesus to the entire world—and even to the angels in heaven. Such a God-given mission of the church should cause us to stand in awe, in amazement, in gratitude—and also call us to action.

We might open our home for Bible study to women from the neighborhood or host neighborhood coffees where the gospel is presented. We might decide to become more bold in witnessing to lost individuals or increase our monetary giving in support of our missionaries. Or we might enlarge our scope of prayer. We might seek out ways we could become personally involved in lives of people in need within our community, such as crisis pregnancy or latchkey programs for children who have no one at home to receive them after school. Always we will pray that God would use us to make a difference in their lives. When we become serious about telling the good news of Jesus to the entire world, God will begin to open unheard-of doors for witness and ministry. My prayer is that none of us will miss that blessing.

Paul adds a personal word in verse 13, encouraging the readers not to be discouraged because of his suffering. He tries to help them understand progress is being made in sharing the good news with the Gentiles; therefore, Ephesian Christians should glory in that progress.

IV. In Prayer (14-21)

In Ephesians 1, we studied a model prayer by Paul. In Ephesians 3 we find another prayer by Paul for the Ephesians. In verse 14 Paul seems to resume a thought he interrupted in verse 1. Reflecting on God's grace in sending Jesus also to the Gentiles ("For this reason") moves Paul to prayer, one of God's great gifts to His children.

You and I have the privilege of talking with and listening to God, our Creator. Not only is prayer a privilege, but God encourages us to pray.

My first lessons in prayer came from my mother, who believed nothing was too great nor too small to take to God in prayer. One fall afternoon Mom and I raked up bushels and bushels of leaves which had fallen from the trees in our yard. While eating supper, I realized a small ring I had worn for several years was no longer on my finger. Mom immediately led us in prayer, asking God for His help in finding the ring, according to His will.

After supper, with flashlight in hand, the two of us returned to the several-foot-high pile of leaves to search for the lost ring. We turned over bushel after bushel of leaves. Suddenly the flashlight's beam revealed a tiny object surrounded by leaves—my ring. I was ecstatic! Again Mom led us in prayer. This time she thanked God for His goodness in allowing us to find the ring.

I am grateful for those first lessons in prayer, for they have laid a foundation in my trusting God for praying about far more serious matters than a child's lost ring.

A study of prayer throughout the Bible is a rewarding one. Repeatedly we find assurances that God wants us to talk with Him, such as is found in Jeremiah 33:3: "Call to me and I will answer you and tell you great and unsearchable things you do not know."

A. Position for Prayer (14)

"For this reason I kneel before the Father" (Eph. 3:14).

No specific position of the body is necessary to talk with and listen to God. We can pray as we sit, stand, or lie down—with our eyes wide open. However, there seems to come a sense of unusual urgency and awe and reverence as we kneel in prayer. This seems to be the attitude of Paul as he kneels before the Father.

B. Specific Prayers for Us, the Church (15-19)

1. That Our Hearts Will Be a Suitable Place in Which Christ Can Live (15-17*a*)

*"From whom his whole family in heaven and on earth derives its name. I pray that out of his glorious riches he may strengthen you with power through his Spirit in your inner being, so that Christ may dwell in your hearts through faith" (Eph. 3:15-17*a).*

God, the Father, is the beginning of all family life both in heaven and on earth. Paul asks that God, from His overflowing riches and ability, would strengthen members of the Ephesian church with His spiritual power within their inner beings. What does this mean?

Barclay explains that the Greeks understood "the inner man" to mean three things:

(1) A person's reason. Paul wants the Ephesians to be better able to distinguish between right and wrong.

(2) A person's conscience. Consciences can become dull. Paul asks God to help the Ephesians to keep their consciences tender toward Him, always sensitive to His leadership and correction.

(3) A person's will. Wills can become weak. Paul asks that God will give the Ephesians the ability to carry through on impressions received from God.[3]

For today's woman "the inner man" means her reason, her conscience, and her will. When through faith our "inner man" is strengthened, Christ will have an adequate place in which He can live permanently.

2. That We Will Understand God's Love (17*b*-19*a*)

"And I pray that you, being rooted and established in love, may have power, together with all the saints, to grasp how wide and long and high and deep is

83

the love of Christ, and to know this love that surpasses knowledge" (Eph. 3:17b-19a).

Paul continues to pray for the Ephesian Christians, asking God to help them to be rooted and established in love. *Rooted* and *established* have taken on new meaning as my husband and I have attempted to landscape our backyard. In early summer we planted four beautiful trailing crape myrtles. Several months later, two of the plants are blooming beautifully. The other two are dry and brittle in spite of the fact all have received the same care.

Why the difference? The last two, evidently, were not in the soil long enough before searing hot Texas winds and 100-plus degree weather attacked them. Their root systems did not become well established.

Paul knows that Christians too can dry up and not accomplish their purpose in life if they are not rooted and well established in Christ's love "as a preparation and condition of understanding the transcendent love of God expressing itself actively in Christ Jesus."[4] In addition, Paul asks God to help the Ephesians to have power to comprehend the dimensions of God's love:

- •Width—God's love includes every person in the world.
- •Length—God's love extends through all time.
- •Height—God's love stretches from earth to heaven.
- •Depth—God's love reaches to the lowest level of human need.

Notice in verse 18 the phrase "together with all the saints." Where can one better comprehend the dimensions of God's love than by being "together" with true believers (saints) in the loving fellowship of a church? Being active in the middle of this kind of loving fellowship enables a Christian to better see the different facets of God's love. What a privilege!

Not only is Paul asking God to help the Ephesians to comprehend the vast dimensions of God's love, but he also asks that they experience (*know*) God's love, which really goes beyond any human's ability to understand.

A modern-day example may help to illustrate this truth. A young woman offered to teach English as a second language to a Brazilian woman who had recently moved into the community. As Andrea talked with the newcomer through an interpreter, the Brazilian woman could hardly believe the American would not charge her a fee. When she asked for a reason, Andrea replied, "Because God loves you, and I do too." A look of utter disbelief was registered on the foreigner's face. She simply could not understand love like that.

3. That We Will Experience the Fullness of God (19*b*)
"That you may be filled to the measure of all the fullness of God" (Eph. 3:19b).

This seems to be the climax of Paul's prayer. What could a Christian desire more than to be filled with the fullness of God? Vaughan comments, "His [Paul's] prayer is that his readers may experience to the extent of their capacity the totality of blessings God is willing and able to bestow . . . that their whole being may be filled with God's presence and power, so that there shall be no room for more."[5] He likens this to the teacup on a seashore being filled over and over again by incoming rolling waves.

C. Conclusion of the Prayer (20-21)

"Now to him who is able to do immeasurably more than all we ask or imagine, according to his power that is at work within us, to him be glory in the church and in Christ Jesus throughout all generations, for ever and ever! Amen" (Eph. 3:20-21).

Paul's prayer stretches our minds and our hearts. He realizes that try as hard as he might, he just has not painted an adequate word picture of God and His love. And in conclusion, he lifts his heart in adoration and praise of God, Who can do more—so much more—than anyone ever dreamed possible. We can imagine his praise escalates as Paul prays that throughout the ages the church and Jesus—ever united as body and head—will bring glory to God.

And with a sudden start, we realize that Paul is including us—all women who are in the church today: that we might bring glory to God through our individual lives and collectively as we serve Him through our churches.

In summary, Paul has served as a prototype, an original example, of a new creation in four ways: (1) in discerning the mystery of God; (2) in receiving God's grace; (3) in understanding God's eternal purpose for His church; and (4) in prayer. Truly he was a new creation with a worldview.

Oh, women of today, we too are new creations if we have allowed Jesus to live within our hearts. Let's determine we will not live our lives on a low, worldly plane, but that we will live in such a way so as not to limit God in what He wants to do in and through us—His body, His church!

For Your Reflection

1. Write here your understanding of the word *mystery* to which Paul refers in this chapter.

2. What one idea or Scripture verse, above all others, captured your attention? Write it here.

3. If you did not write a Scripture verse, write in the space provided Ephesians 3:17*b*-19*a*, committing it to memory.

4. Write the four ways in which Paul showed himself to be a new creation prototype.

5. Place a check mark by one in which you want to experience more growth. Ask God to guide you, showing ways in which you can make progress in that selected area.

---

[1] *New International Version Disciple's Study Bible* (Nashville: Holman Bible Publishers, 1988), 1507.
[2] Geoffrey Barraclough, ed., *The Christian World* (New York: Harry N. Abrams, Inc., 1981), 46.
[3] William Barclay, *The Letters to the Galatians and Ephesians,* The Daily Study Bible Series, rev. ed. (Edinburgh: Saint Andrew Press, 1983), 131.
[4] W. O. Carver, *Ephesians: The Glory of God in the Christian Calling* (1949; reprint, Nashville: Broadman Press, 1979), 113.
[5] Curtis Vaughan, *Ephesians, A Study Guide Commentary* (Grand Rapids: Zondervan Publishing House, 1977), 83.

4. My Place in God's Church

In the first three chapters of Ephesians Paul has dealt with great Christian truths and the place of the church in God's purpose. In Ephesians 4 we look more closely at our place in God's church as instruments to carry out His purpose. Notice the emphasis on *being* as well as on *doing*. The church is not a building, but a fellowship of born-again believers in Jesus.

The church was founded by Jesus Himself. A quick look at Matthew 16 reminds us that Simon Peter, in sharing his idea of Who Jesus was, said, "You are the Christ, the Son of the living God" (Matt. 16:16). Jesus immediately replied, "On this rock [that is, this declaration of Who Jesus is] I will build my church" (Matt. 16:18).

As believers in Jesus Christ, we seek out others who share our beliefs to form a church. Notice Paul's emphasis in both the beginning and the close of this chapter on *being Christlike*. The church may be likened to a laboratory in which we are nurtured toward being authentic, mature Christians.

But membership in God's church also requires us *to do something*. God has placed within each of us a spiritual gift, or gifts, which He expects us to use in helping to build up His church.

Women of today, a worthy goal for us is to achieve and maintain a healthy balance between *being* and *doing*.

I. Live Out the Christian Virtues (1-2)
"As a prisoner for the Lord, then, I urge you to live a life worthy of the calling you have received" (Eph. 4:1).

Paul again refers to his being in prison. From that confinement he offers specific suggestions as to how the Ephesians (and we) may be worthy of the calling as Christians.

A. Humility and Gentleness (2a)
"Be completely humble and gentle" (Eph. 4:2a).

Webster defines *humble* as "not proud or haughty." Jesus modeled humility by leaving the riches of heaven and coming to earth to live the life of a human (Phil. 2:8). He modeled humility when he washed the feet of

His disciples (John 13:2-17).

Barclay describes the gentle person as "the man who is so God-controlled that he is always angry at the right time but never angry at the wrong time."[1]

The gentle woman is considerate of the feelings of others with whom she relates. The humble woman does not demand personal recognition; she serves unselfishly.

B. Patience and Forbearance (2a)

"Be patient, bearing with one another in love" (Eph. 4:2b).

Patience means making allowances for one another because of love for one another.

Jan and Babs served as leaders in women's work of their church. In time, their personalities began to rub against one another.

Feeling insecure at first, Babs often called Jan for reassurance. Irritated by the frequent calls, Jan confided in Rachel, her leader, "If that woman calls me one more time!" Meanwhile, Babs also confided in Rachel she felt Jan was not wholeheartedly supportive of her.

Prayerfully, Rachel wrote a personal note to each woman expressing appreciation for her giftedness and service. She encouraged each to be patient with the other while taking advantage of this opportunity to experience more deeply God's unconditional love.

Today Jan and Babs work happily, and with a heightened sense of respect and appreciation for each other, because each allowed God's Spirit to guide in "bearing with one another in love."

II. Keep Unity of the Spirit (3-6)

"Make every effort to keep the unity of the Spirit through the bond of peace. There is one body and one Spirit—just as you were called to one hope when you were called—one Lord, one faith, one baptism; one God and Father of all, who is over all and through all and in all" (Eph. 4:3-6).

W. O. Carver writes, "The Holy Spirit is working within the entire Body and in each of its members to effect, maintain, and perfect the unity of the whole. Christians are called upon to unite with the Spirit and with one another to the same end."[2]

We are living in a day of divisions and factions in our churches. While differences may appear on the outside, Paul lists seven foundational ideals through which the Spirit can bring true unity on the inside among believers:

(1) One Body—The church, the body of Christ, which is made up of all of God's people.

(2) One Spirit—The Holy Spirit, Who enters our lives when we open our hearts to Jesus, energizes the church.

(3) One Hope—The expectation that God's purpose in bringing together all peoples under the headship of Jesus will become a reality. He no longer wants divisions among peoples and churches.

(4) One Lord—Jesus Christ. He must be our Lord and Lord of all things. Few of us are called on today to denounce Jesus as Lord, but many early Christians gave up their lives rather than deny Him. One such martyr was Polycarp, ancient bishop of Smyrna (now Izmir, Turkey), who was directed to curse Christ. He replied, "For 86 years I have been serving Him, and He has done no wrong to me. How then dare I blaspheme my King Who has saved me?"

(5) One Faith—The common experience all believers have who place their trust in Jesus.

(6) One Baptism—In the early days of Christianity only one mode of baptism was practiced—immersion (Rom. 6:4). "One baptism" refers to the outward experience to testify to the newness of life inside the believer.

(7) One God—This series of "unities" is climaxed with "One God." "God and Father of all" here refers to Father of all believers. "Who is over all" means that God is supreme; there is no one over Him. "Through all" means that God controls and sustains everything. The last phrase, "in all," means that God's powerful presence is felt everywhere.

Paul makes a strong appeal for unity through these sevenfold foundations and the relation of God to all the people in the church, Christ's body.

III. Contribute to My Church's Growth (7-16)
A. Acknowledge Gift of Grace in Every Member (7-10)
Vaughan reminds all church members of their responsibility to perform two ministries: (1) missionary ministry through the church to the world and (2) each member helping her church to grow.[3]

"But to each one of us grace has been given as Christ apportioned it. This is what it says:

> *'When he ascended on high,*
> *he led captives in his train*
> *and gave gifts to men.'*

(What does 'he ascended' mean except that he also descended to the lower, earthly regions? He who descended is the very one who ascended higher than all the heavens, in order to fill the whole universe.)" (Eph. 4:7-10).

Each member within the church has been given a gift by God. The person who says she has nothing to contribute to the building up of her church has not understood God's Word at this point. God has given to each a gift of grace.

The words in parentheses are a reference to Psalm 68:18 in which God, the Victor, returns from battle with captives and gifts. Paul may have used another translation, or adjusted the words for his purpose, for he writes here that Christ "gave gifts to men" while Psalm 68 states "received gifts from men." This means that Christ gave to His followers the gifts He had won through His personal death and victory—grace to all.

B. Recognize God's Provision for Church Growth (11-13)

As we continue to determine our place in God's church, it is comforting to realize God has divinely provided for church growth through gifting each one of us.

1. God Gives Spiritual Gifts to Each Member (11)

"It was he who gave some to be apostles, some to be prophets, some to be evangelists, and some to be pastors, and teachers" (Eph. 4:11).

In addition to gifts mentioned here, other listings are found in Romans 12:4-8; 1 Corinthians 12:7-11, 28-31; 1 Peter 4:10-11. Aside from these special gifts, all believers, filled with God's Spirit, evidence in their lives the fruit of the Spirit (Gal. 5:22-23).

Nowhere is there a complete listing of spiritual gifts. Bible scholars disagree as to whether or not those listed are only representative of total gifts today. As we look carefully at this Ephesian passage, we see that God has provided spiritual gifts necessary for building His church. Here Paul mentions several used to equip "the saints":

- Apostles—In the strictest sense individuals who had seen Jesus; were witnesses of His resurrection; and had been sent out by Him. However, others, such as Paul and Barnabas, were also called apostles.
- Prophets—Individuals who spoke messages they received from the Holy Spirit, going from one church to another to tell them the will of God.
- Evangelists—Individuals called to directly proclaim the gospel.
- Pastor—Shepherd of the church. This office seems to be more permanent than itinerant.
- Teacher—Instructor of the faith. Since printing had not yet been invented, a teacher was necessary to help believers learn about Jesus and what He expected of them.

Many writers agree that the first two spiritual gifts (apostles and prophets) disappeared after books in the New Testament appeared. Some scholars feel that *pastor* and *teacher* combine the two functions into one.

A growing number of women today are becoming interested in discovering their spiritual gifts. Charts and books are available to help a woman determine those gifts. Fortunate is the woman who not only discovers her spiritual gift, but who also learns to use it productively. The book *Yours for the Giving* by Barbara Joiner offers a three-pronged approach to discovering spiritual gifts: (1) biblical study of the gifts; (2) personal identification of gifts; and (3) ways in which an individual may use her gifts within her own church to help build up that body of Christ.

2. God Gives Gifts for a Purpose (12-13)

"To prepare God's people for works of service, so that the body of Christ may be built up until we all reach unity in the faith and in the knowledge of the Son of God and become mature, attaining to the whole measure of the fullness of Christ" (Eph. 4:12-13).

90

Evelyn is a leader to whom God has given many gifts. Using her gifts in women's work has made a distinct contribution toward building up the women, which enhances the growth of the entire church. With a sparkle in her eye, she testifies, "Serving God in this way is the most rewarding thing I have ever done!" Discovering and using one's gifts in the church bring unexpected happiness in addition to spiritual growth.

Upon discovering our gifts, we are called by God to use those gifts in building up the church. We are to come together in unity of the faith. We are to increase in our accurate knowledge about Jesus. We are to become mature. Our goal is to be filled with all of Christ.

Barclay concludes this section with, "The aim of the Church is that her members should reach a stature which can be measured by the fullness of Christ. The aim of the Church is nothing less than to produce men and women who have in them the reflection of Jesus Christ himself."[4]

C. Evaluate My Maturity (14-16)

The word *then* means that if we have attained the aim mentioned in verses 11-13, we should see maturity in three ways: (1) stability in doctrine, (2) speaking the truth in love, and (3) faithfully fulfilling my role in the church.

1. Stability in Doctrine (14)

"Then we will no longer be infants, tossed back and forth by the waves, and blown here and there by every wind of teaching and by the cunning and craftiness of men in their deceitful scheming" (Eph. 4:14).

Women are living in a day when religious appeals come from many different sources. Television and bookstores are flooded with religious programs and books. Some stand in direct contrast to others. What should a woman believe?

One mark of a woman's maturity is that she is well grounded in Jesus, no longer moving from dogma to dogma. She avoids any religion which does not place Jesus in the very center of that faith. Not only has she had a personal encounter with Jesus, but she has become a student of the Bible to determine what the Bible says about God's purpose and her place in it.

2. Speaking the Truth in Love (15)

"Instead, speaking the truth in love, we will in all things grow up into him who is the Head, that is, Christ" (Eph. 4:15).

"Speaking the truth in love" is a challenge, especially for some women like me who grew up in the South. I was taught to try to be tactful in my dealings with others.

One adjustment I experienced while living in middle Europe was hearing the shocking (to me) boldness by which some European women communicated. However, while living in that environment I began to ask God to help me really speak the truth in love. From much prayer and meditation I came to realize my so-called tactfulness might not always be really truthful. I did not intend to be dishonest, but a heavy emphasis on tact sometimes overshadowed absolute honesty.

Stark boldness seems to be at one end of the spectrum while total tactfulness is at the other. Somewhere in between is the Christian's position: Be careful to speak the truth, but also give attention to how that truth might affect another person. Why bother with this? It's because as Christians we are to show our love to others.

I am grateful for my southern heritage, for my European sisters, and for God's Spirit helping me as I seek His balance in "speaking the truth in love" so I may "grow up" into Christ.

3. Faithfully Filling My Role in the Church (16)

"From him the whole body, joined and held together by every supporting ligament, grows and builds itself up in love, as each part does its work" (Eph. 4:16).

What a beautiful word picture Paul paints of a church! As each one of us, gifted by God, finds and fills our role in His church, we are joined with other such believers—all being held together in love by Christ, the Head. Vaughan adds, "The thought is that each Christian is a point of supply for the body of Christ, a channel to receive and pass on life from Christ."[5] Each woman has a responsibility in doing her part to ensure a healthy body of Christ.

IV. Realize I Am Created to Be Like God (17-24)

Made in His image, saved by His Son, empowered by His Spirit, women of today are created to be like God. Does this stretch our minds? *Bist du ein Christ?* is German for "Are you a Christian?" Translated literally, the words mean "Are you a Christ?" I immediately recoil from such perfection, recognizing my own humanity.

Yet, isn't this what God wants us to be? Like Him? Don't we want our lives to be so godly that when people see us, they instead see Jesus and what He is doing in and through us? We are created to be like God. Moving toward this ideal calls for us to separate ourselves from our past pagan days.

A. Break from My Past (17-19)

"So I tell you this, and insist on it in the Lord, that you must no longer live as the Gentiles do, in the futility of their thinking. They are darkened in their understanding and separated from the life of God because of the ignorance that is in them due to the hardening of their hearts. Having lost all sensitivity, they have given themselves over to sensuality so as to indulge in every kind of impurity, with a continual lust for more" (Eph. 4:17-19).

Notice the specific ways in which Christians are to be separated from their evil past: (1) futile thinking—without a purpose; (2) darkened understanding—no discernment; (3) separated from God—never having access to His presence; (4) hardened hearts—stony hearts closed to God and knowledge; (5) lost sensitivity—without feeling; (6) active sensuality—lewd conduct which shocks individuals; (7) every kind of impurity—and with a lust for more. This person has such a desire to get what she wants she does not care how she hurts someone in the getting. She does not even recognize she is sinning, and she lusts for even more.

B. Follow the Truths of Jesus (20-24)

"You, however, did not come to know Christ that way. Surely you heard of him and were taught in him in accordance with the truth that is in Jesus. You were taught, with regard to your former way of life, to put off your old self, which is being corrupted by its deceitful desires; to be made new in the attitude of your minds; and to put on the new self, created to be like God in true righteousness and holiness" (Eph. 4:20-24).

Three truths from Jesus for Christians surface in this passage: (1) put off the old life—this life is dead when one comes to Christ; (2) be made new in your minds—in contrast to the purposelessness of mind mentioned in verse 17; and (3) put on the new life—the righteousness and holiness which God gives.

V. Live as a Christian—Not Just on Sundays (25-32)

"Therefore each of you must put off falsehood and speak truthfully to his neighbor, for we are all members of one body. 'In your anger do not sin': Do not let the sun go down while you are still angry, and do not give the devil a foothold. He who has been stealing must steal no longer, but must work, doing something useful with his own hands, that he may have something to share with those in need.

"Do not let any unwholesome talk come out of your mouths, but only what is helpful for building others up according to their needs, that it may benefit those who listen. And do not grieve the Holy Spirit of God, with whom you were sealed for the day of redemption. Get rid of all bitterness, rage and anger, brawling and slander, along with every form of malice. Be kind and compassionate to one another, forgiving each other, just as in Christ God forgave you" (Eph. 4:25-32).

Paul continues to offer very practical suggestions as to how the Ephesians (and we) need to live and relate with one another. Notice these specific ways:

- Speak truthfully with your neighbor.—Never use falsehoods.
- Do not sin in your anger.—Paul is not saying never get angry, but rather do not sin. He cautions us to direct our anger to the right target, thus avoiding sin. Delaying time in reconciliation can intensify the anger and give the devil a greater opportunity to influence us.
- Make a contribution through useful work.—Paul teaches the Ephesians (and us) not to steal, but to find reputable work to meet our own needs and also to share with people in need.
- Speak only helpfully.—Before a person's conversion, she may have been careless in her words, often becoming foul-mouthed. Paul is urging Christians (and us) not to slip back into our old patterns of speech.
- Do not grieve the Holy Spirit.—The Apostle realizes that at any point where we might slip away from Christian ideals we will grieve God's Spirit.
- Rid self of bitterness, rage, anger, brawling, slander, malice.—Bitterness

means a sour attitude refusing reconciliation. Rage is sudden outburst, while anger is long, misdirected emotion—both of which have no place in a Christian's life. Brawling, slander, and malice—loud talking, insulting language, spiteful words—are out of place as well.

• Be kind.—Paul emphasizes the need for Christians to think as much of the other person's welfare as her own.

• Forgive others.—Notice the model Christians have in knowing how to forgive: Jesus Himself Who has forgiven you and me of our sins. Such quality of forgiveness should characterize our lives.

Women of today, as we discover our place in Christ's church, let us allow God's Spirit to teach us through this chapter. In so doing, our church will become a healthy body of Christ and make its greatest contribution to God's eternal purpose.

For Your Reflection

1. Write the idea or Scripture verse which impressed you most from this chapter.

2. If you did not select a Scripture verse, memorize Ephesians 4:1.

3. Identify your spiritual gift(s).*

4. Write in this space how you are using your gift(s) to help build up your church.

*If you have not identified your spiritual gift, consult your church media library for suggestions or see *Uniquely Gifted* (Discovering Your Spiritual Gifts) by Stuart Calvert (available through Christian bookstores).

---

[1]William Barclay, *The Letters to the Galatians and Ephesians,* The Daily Study Bible Series, rev. ed. (Edinburgh: Saint Andrew Press, 1983), 138.
[2]W. O. Carver, *Ephesians: The Glory of God in the Christian Calling* (1949; reprint, Nashville: Broadman Press, 1979), 118.
[3]Curtis Vaughan, *Ephesians, A Study Guide Commentary* (Grand Rapids: Zondervan Publishing House, 1977), 91.
[4]Barclay, *The Letters to the Galatians and Ephesians,* 150.
[5]Vaughan, *Ephesians,* 97.

5. My Place in Marriage

Singles, before you turn away from this chapter because of its title, let me encourage you to study it carefully. Not until you reach verse 21 does the passage focus specifically on relationships in marriage. Studying the entire chapter should give you practical suggestions to enhance your desire to grow as a Christian. And reading the section on marriage should give you insights into what God expects in a Christian marriage.

The first part of this chapter is written to all Christians, whether married or single. While marriage was planned by God for most adults, it was also His plan for many singles to find great joy and genuine fulfillment in serving God. As we try to discover the meaning of verses 1-20 for our lives, let us realize these concepts speak to every Christian, both single and married people.

I. Live a Life of Love (1-2)

"Be imitators of God, therefore, as dearly loved children and live a life of love, just as Christ loved us and gave himself up for us as a fragrant offering and sacrifice to God" (Eph. 5:1-2).

Paul suggests we are to be imitators of God. Thomas à Kempis, a fourteenth-century German Augustinian canon, wrote *The Imitation of Christ* to give guidance in following Christ's example. "It has become the best-loved Christian book ever written and its continuing popularity is second only to that of the Bible."[1]

Often today we hear Christians speak more of letting Christ live through their lives than imitating Him. In any case, God and Christ are our models.

Christ is our model for living a life of love. Notice the depth of this love: willingness to give one's life. The Greek word for this kind of unselfish love is *agape*. For the Christian this love is not optional; Jesus commanded it: "A new command I give you: Love one another. As I have loved you, so you must love one another" (John 13:34). Jesus' love was accepting, forgiving, building others up, and taking the initiative in all of these. This love involves our will.

This, then, is the love we should exhibit in our lives to all people whether we are single or whether we are married. Living within the marriage relationship is an arena where this kind of love must be lived out on a daily basis to achieve greatest happiness.

II. Avoid Any Kind of Impurity (3-7)

"But among you there must not be even a hint of sexual immorality, or of any kind of impurity, or of greed, because these are improper for God's holy people. Nor should there be obscenity, foolish talk or coarse joking, which are out of place, but rather thanksgiving. For of this you can be sure: No immoral, impure or greedy person—such a man is an idolater—has any inheritance in the kingdom of Christ and of God. Let no one deceive you with empty words, for because of such things God's wrath comes on those who are disobedient. Therefore do not be partners with them"(Eph. 5:3-7).

Paul's list of "any kind of impurity" includes: immorality, greed, obscenity ("something disgusting to the senses"), foolish talk, or coarse joking. A person exhibiting this kind of behavior, which gives no evidence of a genuine conversion experience, receives only the wrath of God.

Women of today, we are besieged by the media, as well as by lives around us, with the concept that anything is all right as long as it feels good. But the woman serious about her spiritual growth should avoid any of these things—even a hint of sexual immorality. Paul encourages us to live a life which can be transparent to the world.

III. Live a Life of Light (8-14)

"For you were once darkness, but now you are light in the Lord. Live as children of light (for the fruit of the light consists in all goodness, righteousness and truth) and find out what pleases the Lord. Have nothing to do with the fruitless deeds of darkness, but rather expose them. For it is shameful even to mention what the disobedient do in secret. But everything exposed by the light becomes visible, for it is light that makes everything visible. This is why it is said:

> *'Wake up, O sleeper,*
> *rise from the dead,*
> *and Christ will shine on you'" (Eph. 5:8-14).*

The Apostle Paul encourages all believers, single or married, to live as children who have received in our lives Jesus, the Light of the world.

Notice three ideas: (1) "live as children of light" (v. 8)—our behavior should reflect commitment to Christ; (2) produce fruit of the light (v. 9)—goodness, righteousness, and truth should come from our lives; and (3) expose the "fruitless deeds of darkness" (v. 11)—not only should we "not have anything to do with" them, but we should turn God's light on them to expose them. Through His power, then, we are able to live as His children in a world filled with darkness.

The final verse may be related to Isaiah 60:1, or it may have been words from a baptismal hymn sung by early Christians. It can be a reminder to nonbelievers to wake up and let Jesus' light shine on them.

This passage may also be a reminder to us women to wake up to what is happening around us. May we live so like Jesus that others in seeing our lives are impressed with what Jesus is doing in and through us, shedding His light on the darkness of our world.

IV. Be Filled with God's Spirit (15-20)

"Be very careful, then, how you live—not as unwise but as wise, making the most of every opportunity, because the days are evil. Therefore do not be foolish, but understand what the Lord's will is. Do not get drunk on wine, which leads to debauchery. Instead, be filled with the Spirit. Speak to one another with psalms, hymns and spiritual songs. Sing and make music in your heart to the Lord, always giving thanks to God the Father for everything, in the name of our Lord Jesus Christ" (Eph. 5:15-20).

This passage mentions three do nots: (1) do not live unwisely; (2) do not be foolish; and (3) do not get drunk on wine.

In contrast, suggestions are given for positive actions: (1) live wisely, making the most of every opportunity; (2) understand God's will; (3) speak to each other with the Scriptures and spiritual songs; (4) sing and make music; and (5) give thanks to God for everything.

Henry Blackaby comments on understanding God's will: "I have found in my own life that I can release the way to Him. Then I take care of everything He tells me one day at a time. He gives me plenty to do to fill each day with meaning and purpose. If I do everything He says, I will be in the center of His will when He wants to use me for a special assignment."[2]

The key to being able to live wisely is found in verse 18, "be filled with the Spirit." God's Spirit comes to live within us when we open our hearts to Jesus. As we empty our lives of sin and ask God to be Lord of our lives, we are filled with His Spirit. However, anytime we sin, we must ask forgiveness from God so that our hearts might be clean. This process is described in 1 John 1:9. The verb "be filled" is not a onetime action, but is continuous. "The 'filling' is different from the baptism in/with/by the Spirit. The latter is experienced by all believers and is never repeated (cf. 1 Cor. 12:13)."[3]

Again these words apply to women who are single and also to those in a marriage relationship. However, in verses 21-33 Paul turns his attention to individuals who are married.

V. Meet Each Other's Needs (21)

This is being written on our 36th wedding anniversary. I wish I could communicate to you the depth of love my husband and I know and the joy we experience living together. Every year has gotten better because we believe the statement by William Barclay, "In Christian marriage there are not two partners, but three—and the third is Christ."[4]

Don't misunderstand—we also make mistakes; we have our difficulties, our differences, and ups and downs. As we have offered even our mistakes up to God, He has used many of them to draw us closer to Him and to each other. Learning from those difficulties has helped our marriage to grow stronger.

What is the secret of a happy, permanent marriage? I think we have discovered that secret as we have come to realize that marriage itself was created by God for man and woman's greatest happiness as they assume their place in God's purpose. Trying to live out God's principles for marriage, such as are found in this passage, ensures a depth of happiness that can be experienced in no other way.

Paul writes in verse 21, *"Submit to one another out of reverence for Christ."*

The phrase "out of reverence for Christ" in some Bible translations comes at the beginning of the sentence. Each person is made in the image of God (Gen. 1:26). Therefore, part of our loving each other is to have respect for our mate, the person created in the image of God, Whom we reverence.

Billy Graham shares his insights: "In Ephesians we . . . read that wives are to defer to their husbands, to submit to their husbands [v. 22]. What does that mean? Well, when one loves it is easy to defer, it is easy to submit. But let me tell you something else: Husbands are to submit to their wives. You don't hear that very often, do you? Ephesians 5:21 says, 'Submitting yourselves one to another in the fear of God.' We are to submit ourselves with love in the fear of the Lord."[5]

My husband and I feel that verse 21 is the foundation of mutuality in marriage. Each partner shares in the responsibilities of marriage and also in its joys. One might paraphrase verse 21 to read, "Out of reverence for Christ, meet each other's needs."

Countless marriages have failed because the partners have not met each others' needs. Too often selfishness has reared its ugly head to insist that one's own needs must be met, forgetting Christian marriage calls for meeting needs of the mate. And in the meeting of the other's needs, one's own needs usually are met.

Some partners spend years in the marriage relationship without identifying each other's needs or in loving conversation as they share how each might help the other in meeting those needs. An inordinate amount of time spent in caring for their children or given to work outside the home often causes neglect of the primary concern, under God: caring for one's mate.

Meeting each other's needs does not mean that couples become absorbed only in each other. Rather, in this process, both look in the same direction to God, to seek ways of glorifying Him. Because our needs are being met, our experience is that we can serve God more effectively.

VI. Understand Husband/Wife Roles in Marriage (22-33)

When one of our sons was a teenager, I asked him to help with something in the kitchen. "That's woman's work," he quickly replied. Years ago roles of women and men were more fixed than they are now. Today many married couples assess the abilities each has to determine what responsibilities each will carry in the home. How one couple envisions their responsibilities may be different from the way another couple perceives theirs. Many of these responsibilities can be very flexible. However, God's Word gives enduring principles, which when followed can ensure great happiness in marriages today.

A. Role of the Wife (22-24)

"Wives, submit to your husbands as to the Lord. For the husband is the head of the wife as Christ is the head of the church, his body, of which he is the Savior. Now as the church submits to Christ, so also wives should submit to their husbands in everything" (Eph. 5:22-24).

For many people today the word *submit* is not in their vocabulary. However, as Christians, first of all we should be submissive to God and His will for our lives. And when a Christian chooses to marry, she tries to discover and live out God's instructions found in God's Word. Let us explore further the meaning of *submit* in a Christian context.

"Wives, submit to your husbands," does not mean wives are to become doormats or are to be controlled and ordered around by a husband interested only in having his own needs met. Personally, I have no problem submitting (deferring) to my husband, who I know loves me in an unselfish way and who has also submitted his life to Christ. (Reread Billy Graham's words on submission on p. 98.)

The wife's role, then, calls for her to be voluntarily submissive to her husband, as to the Lord. This is part of her Christian duty. She also recognizes that her husband is to be head of the wife as Christ is of the church. Any unit needs a head: a committee has a chairman; a corporation has a president; and God's Word indicates that the husband is head of the wife, also implying head of the family.

Such headship does not conflict with the idea of mutuality mentioned in this section. For example, a husband and wife confer on a certain matter. If they cannot make a clear-cut decision, it would seem that the husband as head of the wife/family must make the final decision. But notice, the husband has the responsibility for making the kind of decision which will be best for both of them and the family. This is not license for him to be authoritative, to have his own way, but an opportunity to exercise his servanthood in deciding what is best for them all under God.

B. Role of the Husband (25-33)

"Husbands, love your wives, just as Christ loved the church and gave himself up for her to make her holy, cleansing her by the washing with water through the word, and to present her to himself as a radiant church, without stain or wrinkle or any other blemish, but holy and blameless. In this same way, husbands ought to love their wives as their own bodies. He who loves his wife loves himself. After all, no one ever hated his own body, but he feeds and cares for it, just as Christ does the church—for we are members of his body. For this reason a man will leave his father and mother and be united to his wife, and the two will become one flesh. This is a profound mystery—but I am talking about Christ and the church. However, each one of you also must love his wife as he loves himself, and the wife must respect her husband"(Eph. 5:25-33).

Several times in this one section Paul states that husbands should love their wives. The kind of love to which Paul refers is not the usual kind of romantic love we speak about so casually these days. This love is agape, "a higher form of love, a deliberate attitude of mind that concerns itself with the well-being of the one loved."[6] When a wife is loved in this way, she has no problem being subject to her husband.

Paul describes how husbands are to love their wives: (1) as Christ loved the church (vv. 25-27); (2) as they love themselves (v. 28); and (3) above all other human relationships (v. 31).

First, in verses 25-27 we note Christ loved the church so much that He gave up His life for it. Husbands should love their wives so much they would be willing to give up their lives for them. Paul moves away from his discussion of marriage as he describes why Christ gave His life for the church. Through His sacrifice the church is to become holy—set apart— and blameless, cleansed from sin; and presented to Him in all its radiance.

A second way in which a husband should love his wife is as he loves his own body (v. 28). Surely he would not harm his own body in any way, but try to do everything to enhance his body. Such is the love a man should have for his wife.

Third, Paul suggests husbands should love their wives above all other human relationships (v. 31). Here he quotes from Genesis 2:24: "For this reason a man will leave his father and mother and be united to his wife, and they will become one flesh."

When a man marries, he should leave home emotionally. This does not mean he is to cut ties with his home of origin nor continue to love his parents. It does mean he should give primary allegiance under God to his mate rather than to his mother or father. The same is true for the wife.

In closing this passage, Paul teaches that the wife should respect her husband. Respect is another facet of love, unselfish love. And lest one thinks Paul gives women the freedom *not* to love their husbands since this is not mentioned here in describing the role of the wife, we need to look at the total teaching of Paul. In Titus 2:4 Paul encourages the older women to "train the younger women to love their husbands."

Women of today, with divorce rates skyrocketing and promiscuous sexual behavior rampaging throughout our country, what can we do? Let us be sure we are carefully living by God's marriage principles, some of which are given in this letter to the Ephesians. In doing so we are fulfilling our place in God's purpose. Some people today may think following God's plan for marriage is old-fashioned, but marriage partners who live by His principles know for themselves a lifetime of joy unimagined. If you are looking for true, lasting happiness in marriage, don't let the world dictate principles for your marriage; follow God's!

For Your Reflection

1. What idea or Scripture verse impressed you most from this study? Write it here.

2. If you did not select a Scripture verse, memorize Ephesians 5:1.

3. List specific ways in which you can today live as a "child of light" (v. 8).

4. For married women

   A. List three needs of your own you would like for your husband to meet.

   B. Ask your husband to list three needs of his he would like for you to meet.

   C. Set aside time in which the two of you, having identified these three needs, share ways those needs can be met. Incorporate them into your daily routine. Pray together.

---

[1]Veronica Zundel, *Christian Classics* (Oxford, England: Lion Publishing Co., 1985), 43.

[2]Henry Blackaby and Claude King, *Experiencing God* (Nashville: Sunday School Board of the Southern Baptist Convention, 1990), 11.

[3]Curtis Vaughan, *Ephesians, A Study Guide Commentary* (Grand Rapids: Zondervan Publishing House, 1977), 112.

[4]William Barclay, *The Letters to the Galatians and Ephesians,* The Daily Study Bible Series, rev. ed. (Edinburgh: Saint Andrew Press, 1983), 175.

[5]Billy Graham, "10 Commandments for the Home," *Decision,* June 1974, 12.

[6]Vaughan, *Ephesians,* 117.

6. My Place in Other Relationships

Paul moves from a discussion of marriage in chapter 5 to family and other relationships in this last chapter of Ephesians. Let us explore our place in these "other" relationships.

I. In My Family (1-4)
A. Children and Parents (1-3)
"Children, obey your parents in the Lord, for this is right. 'Honor your father and mother'—which is the first commandment with a promise—'that it may go well with you and that you may enjoy long life on the earth'" (Eph. 6:1-3).

Two key words are found here: *obey* and *honor*. Webster defines *obey* as "to follow the commands or guidance of." Notice such obedience is a Christian duty "in the Lord." There is a desperate need in today's society to help children understand their responsibility to obey their parents.

The second key word, part of a child's Christian duty, is found in verse 2 where Paul writes, "Honor your father and mother." Webster defines *honor* as "a showing of merited respect." This primary commandment, which Paul quotes from Exodus 20:12, is valid today. Paul broadens the Old Testament promise of long life in the Promised Land to include all children.

Vaughan comments, "It would be an error, however, to apply Paul's words rigidly, for some who honor their parents die early and others who totally ignore the divine injunction may live to a ripe old age."[1]

B. Parents and Children (4)
"Fathers, do not exasperate your children; instead, bring them up in the training and instruction of the Lord" (Eph. 6:4).

In the preceding chapter mutuality in relationships was established as basic in marriage. The same is true in parent-child relationships. Parents also have a responsibility to their children.

Fathers carry the responsibility for being head of the home (implied in Eph. 5:23). However, in our society children need guidance from both father and mother. *Exasperate* means not to break the spirit of your child. On the other hand, parents have the responsibility to rear children in such a way they will be taught the things of God and led toward the time they too will become Christians. God first nurtures children through their parents. I realize that today a large number of children grow up in single-parent homes. Single mothers, while parenting may be much more difficult for you, God's same principles still apply: Do not break the spirit of your children, and bring them up in the nurture of God. And remember, He promises to be with you always.

II. In the Workplace (5-9)

The theme of mutuality continues in the relationship between slaves and masters. First, attention is given to slaves.

A. Slaves and Masters (5-8)

"Slaves, obey your earthly masters with respect and fear, and with sincerity of heart, just as you would obey Christ. Obey them not only to win their favor when their eye is on you, but like slaves of Christ, doing the will of God from your heart. Serve wholeheartedly, as if you were serving the Lord, not men, because you know that the Lord will reward everyone for whatever good he does, whether he is slave or free" (Eph 6:5-8).

Two key words are noted in the responsibility of slave toward masters: *obey* and *serve*. Notice words Paul adds to reinforce the kind of obedience slaves are to exercise toward their masters: *respect, fear (awe), sincerity*. He calls them to obey their masters just as if they were obeying God whether the master is watching or not.

Also Paul asks that slaves serve their masters as if they were serving God. He reminds them that the Lord will reward all, for all are equal before God.

Something of this spirit is seen when a mother gave last-minute instructions to her young son, leaving for his first job: "Remember, son, your time belongs to your employer. Serve him well."

B. Masters and Slaves (9)

"And masters, treat your slaves in the same way. Do not threaten them, since you know that he who is both their Master and yours is in heaven, and there is no favoritism with him" (Eph. 6:9).

In Paul's day slaves had no rights of their own. Jesus' standard was different (see Gal. 3:28). Masters were to treat their slaves decently and with respect. A reminder is that God in heaven sees all.

The mutuality principle covers relationships in the workplace today as well as in the home. Christians of the twentieth century still have an obligation under God to follow this principle.

Women of today, we know Satan tries to keep us from always living as Christians in our marriage, within our family, in the marketplace, and with all others. Don't despair. God has provided help to enable us to be victorious.

III. In My Victory over Satan (10-18)

A. Know the Source of My Strength (10-11)

"Finally, be strong in the Lord and in his mighty power. Put on the full armor of God so that you can take your stand against the devil's schemes" (Eph. 6:10-11).

Realizing that the devil wants to keep unbelievers from becoming believers and Christians from living the abundant life, God encourages us to be strong in Him and in His power. Keep in mind that the all-powerful God Who created the universe is the same God with Whom we have a personal relationship through Jesus. As we open our hearts to Him, He can strengthen us through His Holy Spirit, Who lives within us (1 John 4:4).

As Paul was writing this section of the letter, he may have become quite conscious of the soldier to whom he was chained. Or he might have thought of Isaiah 59:17. At any rate, he suggests that as we don the whole armor of God, we will be able to stand up against the devil's crafty schemes.

B. Identify My Enemy (12)

"For our struggle is not against flesh and blood, but against the rulers, against the authorities, against the powers of this dark world and against the spiritual forces of evil in the heavenly realms" (Eph 6:12).

This verse gives us a clearer understanding of who our enemy is. The nature of our conflict, "in the heavenly realms," is in the "superphysical realm of thought . . . involving all heavenly interests."[2]

Notice we are not fighting against mere men and women, but against supernatural powers. Paul lists our enemies: rulers, authorities, powers of the dark world, and spiritual forces of evil above. All of these are "invisible powers in rebellion against God."[3]

In Paul's day thinkers organized these enemies into systems far removed from our thought patterns today. Carver suggests we are too far away from their reality, banishing them "from our 'scientific minds'; yet in all the realms of life he [the devil] and they [his helpers] are still rampant and destructive."[4] We would be devastated if we did not know that ultimately God will triumph.

We are keenly aware there is an active power of evil in the world today. Never before have we experienced so much violent crime, so much disregard for law and order, so much destruction of life through drugs and abortion. Few families escape the ravages of the devil's attacks.

If the devil came to us with an evil face, pitchfork, and a long tail, we could immediately recognize him. Unfortunately, this is not how he appears. Rather, he comes to us in an alluring, persuasive manner, striking us at our most vulnerable points. How can we protect ourselves from his onslaughts? God's Word tells us we can prepare for spiritual warfare by wearing His armor, which Paul describes.

C. Dress for Combat (13-18)
1. Put on the Whole Armor (13)

"Therefore put on the full armor of God, so that when the day of evil comes, you may be able to stand your ground, and after you have done everything, to stand" (Eph. 6:13).

Once again Paul instructs us to don the entire armor—not leaving off one single piece. It is as if he is warning us to be ready, for we never know when the enemy will attack ("day of evil"). To be able to stand strong and withstand the devil, we must be ready at all times. First comes the belt.

a) Belt of Truth (14*a*)

"Stand firm, then, with the belt of truth buckled around your waist" (Eph. 6:14a).

In order to stand firm against the devil we must buckle our belt of truth. In the Roman armor the belt not only held together any flowing garment but also gave a sense of stability and security. God's truth for us today does the same thing. His belt of truth means "integrity, consistent devotion of all one's powers, and their integration in undivided coordination. Ethical and moral consistency within the self and with the character and purpose of God is suggested."[5] Inner integrity must accompany the outer armor.

b) Breastplate of Righteousness (14*b*)

"With the breastplate of righteousness in place" (Eph. 6:14b).

In the ancient Roman armor the breastplate was to protect all vital organs. Only God's righteousness can protect our vital organs. Isaiah reminds us that "all our righteous acts are like filthy rags" (64:6). We acquire God's kind of righteousness when we by faith accept Jesus as our Saviour.

c) Shoes of Readiness (15)

"And with your feet fitted with the readiness that comes from the gospel of peace" (Eph. 6:15).

In Paul's day when soldiers put on their sandals, they were ready to travel. When we have received God's peace in our hearts through this personal relationship with Jesus, we too should be ready to travel with a gospel to share with our enemies, "Be reconciled to God" (2 Cor. 5:20b).

d) Shield of Faith (16)

"In addition to all this, take up the shield of faith, with which you can extinguish all the flaming arrows of the evil one" (Eph. 6:16).

This kind of shield for the well-equipped Roman soldier was not a round shield, but large and rectangular, which offered greater protection to his body. Such a shield could ward off the extremely dangerous fire-tipped darts hurled by the enemy.

The Christian's shield, Paul writes, is faith. Notice the sense of security one has that this faith can extinguish *all* flaming darts sent by the devil. One thinks of deadly temptations hurled our way. How wonderful it is to know our shield of faith in God can protect us: "No temptation has seized you except what is common to man. And God is faithful; he will not let you be tempted beyond what you can bear. But when you are tempted, he will also provide a way out so that you can stand up under it" (1 Cor. 10:13).

Temptations, evil spirits, and stray thoughts can never penetrate the shield of faith.

e) Helmet of Salvation (17 a)
"Take the helmet of salvation" (Eph. 6:17a).

A helmet protected the head, location of the control system, of the Roman soldier.

Paul begins this statement with the word *take.* Salvation is offered to us by God through Jesus. We are saved when we receive (take) God's love gift, Jesus.

The meaning here is that we are to be conscious at all times of our salvation.

f) Sword of the Spirit (17 b)
"And the sword of the Spirit, which is the word of God" (Eph. 6:17b).

The sword of the Roman soldier had cutting power. Paul's parallel to the Christian armor is the sword of the Spirit, the word of God, which is "sharper than any double-edged sword" (Heb. 4:12).

Mom grew up in the Roman Catholic faith, but it was not until she heard a Baptist minister preach on John 3:15-16 that she understood her need for a personal relationship with Jesus. It was as if God's Word had pierced her heart when she heard, "Just as Moses lifted up the snake in the desert, so the Son of Man must be lifted up, that everyone who believes in him may have eternal life" (John 3:14-15). That *everyone* included her, and that day she gave her heart to Jesus.

Jesus resisted temptation when He used God's Word (Matt. 4:1-11). Three times Satan tempted Him, and three times Jesus replied with words from God's Word.

Today when we refer to God's Word, we usually mean the Bible. Carver cautions, "The Bible will be the first, most important, the only finally reliable Word of God, if under the guidance and illumination of the Holy Spirit it becomes the revelation of the Personal Word, Jesus Christ, the Son of the Father."[6]

2. Put on the Armor Through Prayer (18)
"And pray in the Spirit on all occasions with all kinds of prayers and requests. With this in mind, be alert and always keep on praying for all the saints" (Eph. 6:18).

Some writers include prayer as one part of the spiritual armor. Carver comments, "It is better to treat it as the attitude and conscious experience of the soul through every stage of his battles and with each use of every weapon of defense and of offense."[7]

It is through prayer, then, we put on the spiritual armor—every piece:

belt of truth; breastplate of righteousness; shoes of readiness; shield of faith; helmet of salvation; and sword of the Spirit.

Notice instructions on prayer in this verse: (1) pray in the Spirit—with His help (Rom. 8:26); (2) on all occasions—times of tremendous needs as well as small ones; (3) with all kinds of prayers and requests—formal, informal, conversational, written, silent, spoken, and all and any kind of request; (4) with alertness—ever be on the lookout for the devil, for he is always eager to distract us; and (5) with persistence in prayer—never giving up—especially for all the saints (believers).

IV. In Praying for Missionaries and Other Leaders (19-20)

"Pray also for me, that whenever I open my mouth, words may be given me so that I will fearlessly make known the mystery of the gospel, for which I am an ambassador in chains. Pray that I may declare it fearlessly, as I should" (Eph. 6:19-20).

In asking for specific prayers, Paul gives a three-faceted suggestion as to how the Ephesians might pray for him: (1) spiritual freedom ("whenever I open my mouth, words may be given me"); (2) boldness ("I will fearlessly make known the mystery of the gospel"); and (3) courage ("declare it . . . as I should"). These three facets—spiritual freedom, boldness, and courage—desperately are needed in our prayers today as we pray for our missionaries and other leaders.

V. Conclusion (21-24)

"Tychicus, the dear brother and faithful servant in the Lord, will tell you everything, so that you also may know how I am and what I am doing. I am sending him to you for this very purpose, that you may know how we are, and that he may encourage you. Peace to the brothers, and love with faith from God the Father and the Lord Jesus Christ. Grace to all who love our Lord Jesus Christ with an undying love" (Eph. 6:21-24).

Tychicus, a trusted companion of Paul (Acts 20:4; Col. 4:7-8; 2 Tim. 4:12), seems to be delivering the letter to give Ephesian Christians a report on Paul and to encourage them.

Paul concludes with a blessing, using great words of the faith—*peace, faith, grace, love.* Paul wants the Ephesian Christians, and us today, increasingly to experience each of these in all their fullness coming from God Himself.

Women of today, as these great concepts fully come to life in our lives, empowered by His Spirit, we can be sure we have found our place in relating with others as well as in God's eternal purpose. But the blessing is not ours alone; it includes all people—all races, all cultures—who love our Lord Jesus with a love that never dies. God invites you and me to actively share His message with lost peoples of the world. In doing so we join Him in carrying out His eternal purpose. What a benediction! What an invitation!

A Final Word to the Reader

Study of these two Pauline letters, Galatians and Ephesians, has been to help us grow spiritually. As we continue to open our hearts to God's Spirit, Who brings to life His words in these letters, may we experience significant growth in freedom to be our best selves in God's purpose. His eternal purpose calls us to be actively involved in the lives of people, always ready to help meet spiritual as well as physical needs. And in so doing may each of us in time "be called oaks of righteousness, a planting of the Lord for the display of his splendor" (Isa. 61:3*b*).

For Your Reflection

1. What idea or Scripture verse impressed you most in chapter 6?

2. If you did not select a Scripture verse, memorize Ephesians 6:10.

3. A. List the elements of the armor for spiritual warfare.

   B. Dress yourself each morning in God's armor.

4. Pray for a missionary, using Ephesians 6:19-20.

5. In two or three sentences write your answer to this question: What is my place in God's purpose?

---

[1] Curtis Vaughan, *Ephesians, A Study Guide Commentary* (Grand Rapids: Zondervan Publishing House, 1977), 120.
[2] W. O. Carver, *Ephesians: The Glory of God in the Christian Calling* (1949; reprint, Nashville: Broadman Press, 1979), 155.
[3] Vaughan, *Ephesians,* 126.
[4] Carver, *The Glory of God in the Christian Calling,* 156.
[5] Ibid., 157.
[6] Ibid., 160.
[7] Ibid.

About the author

Monte M. Clendinning is conference coordinator, World Mission and Evangelism Center, Southwestern Baptist Theological Seminary, Fort Worth, Texas. She is an educator, author, and noted conference leader. A native of Mississippi, Monte is a wife and mother and has served as a foreign missionary to Switzerland.